INCREDIBLE PLANTS

ODDITIES, CURIOSITIES & ECCENTRICITIES

ROBERT LEE BEHME

 Sterling Publishing Co., Inc.   New York

D1227648

Edited by Laurel Ornitz

Library of Congress Cataloging-in-Publication Data

Behme, Robert Lee.
    Incredible plants : oddities, curiosities & eccentricities / Robert
Lee Behme.
        p.   cm.
    Includes index.
    ISBN 0-8069-8244-6
    1. Plants.   I. Title.
QK50.B44   1992
581—dc20   91-38788
                                                                CIP

10   9   8   7   6   5   4   3   2   1

First paperback edition published in 1993 by
Sterling Publishing Company, Inc.
387 Park Avenue South, New York, N.Y. 10016
© 1992 by Robert Lee Behme
Distributed in Canada by Sterling Publishing
% Canadian Manda Group, P.O. Box 920, Station U
Toronto, Ontario, Canada M8Z 5P9
Distributed in Great Britain and Europe by Cassell PLC
Villiers House, 41/47 Strand, London WC2N 5JE, England
Distributed in Australia by Capricorn Link Ltd.
P.O. Box 665, Lane Cove, NSW 2066
Manufactured in the United States of America
All rights reserved

Sterling ISBN 0-8069-8244-6 Trade
              0-8069-8245-4 Paper

CONTENTS

Color section follows page 32.

For Margery

1
IN THE BEGINNING

Nature's amazing plant world is composed of the weird and the wonderful, including nearly every possible shading and variation. Any place you care to point a finger, you chance the unexpected.

At one end of the spectrum are plants that are confirmed meat eaters, because the land where they live lacks essential dietary components. At the other end are those that, lacking roots, live high above ground, surviving on the hard work of others. Somewhere in the middle are thousands of "common" plants, but they also have an exciting story to tell.

Many experts believe that the vast range of plant life is the result of pure chance and accidental evolution—a surprising run of luck if even partially true. But others insist that there is abundant evidence of a substantially more wondrous "plan"—a view a bit more reassuring and every bit as astonishing.

From either scenario, the beginning of earth-bound life was unlikely, and is a story as interesting as any person could contrive.

Moving to Land

In that distant time when our planet was young and developing, much of it was covered by water—which is exactly where life began.

Rudimentary plants unknown in our time were the first living things to make the difficult and challenging transition from water to land. Although the move probably spanned only a few feet, from the shallows of some prehistoric ocean to the swampy shoreline, it was a dramatic step with untold ramifications.

In water, the essentials were within easy reach. Water cradled plant life, gently moving it about, as food floated conveniently by.

Life on land involved several important adaptations:

● Perhaps the most basic was learning to survive in a radically different environment: earth and air, as opposed to water.

- Since water no longer provided support, plants had to either grow flat along the ground or devise some system to hold themselves erect. The first species ashore hugged the land, but in time some developed the sturdy cellular structures we see in stems and trunks, enabling them to rise above the earth and stand tall.
- In the ocean, food was readily available. On land, plants had to find new sources of nourishment and had to devise new ways of obtaining it. As we shall discover, these demands bore a number of unexpected results.
- In water, reproduction took place by means of spores that floated to easy-to-reach partners. On land, plants needed new ways of reproducing and what evolved was a system of readily transportable seeds.
- Seeds had to be pollinated, or made ready to reproduce. Since land-based plants were rooted, the new system had to involve the use of intermediaries—everything from insects to birds. How plants attract and manipulate their pollinators is an intriguing, almost unbelievable part of the story of plant life.

In the Beginning

Life began in the sea. Among the first forms of life we know much about was primitive algae—a form not yet plant or animal. Primitive algae appeared two to three billion years ago, sometime near the end of the first, or Archeozoic, era.

Experts vaguely agree that land vegetation has existed for at least one billion years—twice as long as the existence of rooted plants.

The Spread of Plants

Perhaps the most amazing fact is that from a few successful primitive species that made the leap to land has come an absolutely unbelievable array of life—more than 450,000 different plants at the latest count.

The Importance of Fossils

Our only knowledge of Earth's first land plants comes from fossilized records, actual parts of prehistoric life pressed and preserved in the earth.

Fossil records of land plants begin with the third, or Paleozoic, era, the "Age of Rock." Imprints of prehistoric species from that time not only supply scientists with images of those plants, but they also offer reliable evidence of ancient climates and soils. Together they trace the path of evolution.

From the Pennsylvanian period, which occurred towards the end of the Paleozoic era and ended more than 265 million years ago, we get our first clear picture of rooted plants.

Many land plants can trace their beginnings to a few primitive water species that made the successful transition.

Fossil Records: Earliest Views

People in early civilizations generally believed that fossils were made in their own time by stone-making spirits or other cosmic forces. They thought that fossils were not old at all but were created in current time.

Work of the Gods

Even today people in one mountainous northern region of China believe that the imprints of ancient leaves found in the local shale are not records of prehistoric life.

Locals insist that these imprints are the work of the gods, either their first attempts at drawing or an early kind of writing.

First Recognition

While early civilizations did not recognize the importance of fossils, a limited understanding was shown by the Greeks in the time of Aristotle

(384–322 B.C.). Yet it wasn't until the thirteenth century that the German philosopher and scientist Albertus Magnus gave the world the first written account of the importance of fossil records.

A Flowerless World

There were no flowers among the planet's first plants, and compared with today's trees, ancient species were small and simple.

Tall Ferns

By the end of the Devonian period, in the Paleozoic era, many kinds of fern were taller than the surrounding trees. The planet was covered by prolific shallow-water plants, some reaching heights of 80 to 100 feet.

Plants and Evolution

Early botanists did not believe there were such things as "primitive" plants. Even into the eighteenth century, in the time of Linnaeus, it was believed that all of nature had been created in that first week when God made the Universe, the Earth, and the Garden of Eden.

Eden was known as the most wonderful botanical garden in the world. It was thought that all the plants in the world could have been found there—bright and in full bloom, just as we see them today.

An Early Plant

The first plants surfaced more than 200 million years ago.

One primitive plant, growing on the earth before the arrival of dinosaurs and still in existence, is the cycad, a tropical palmlike evergreen.

Although it doesn't produce a true flower, it is popular with gardeners because of its ornamental palmlike foliage.

Soil

The soil in which most plants grow was not a part of the earth when the world began. It developed over millions of years.

The Carboniferous period, which followed the Devonian, lasted for 35 million years. During that time, mountains arose, marine animals were common, and the first flying insects, actually gigantic creatures, appeared. Soil began forming and accumulating minerals and other elements essential to plant life.

Before this, the earth was a hostile environment. There was no way for nature to gain a foothold.

Bacteria

Bacteria are the oldest and most abundant of nature's soil dwellers.

Types known to scientists as *autotrophic bacteria* have left their traces in rocks for more than a billion years. In prehistoric times they survived by oxidizing rock itself. These were the soil-makers.

They literally converted our young world from uninhabitable hard stuff into something useful, giving us iron, carbon, and other elements. Certain bacteria still function in this way.

Others have evolved and now rely on organic substances.

Early Vegetation

Near the end of the Devonian period, partly because of changes in climate and partly because of chemical changes, the variety and amount of vegetation increased considerably.

Fossil records indicate the development of hundreds of new species. Many were the swamp-growing ancestors of the ferns and mosses we know today.

Oldest Plants

Many of the oldest plants were lost to history hundreds of thousands of years ago and scientists know of most of them only from fossil records. A few species, however, have survived into our time. Among those plants with direct links to early plant life are two groups of nonflowering, rootless plants: mosses and liverworts.

Mosses have rudimentary stems and leaves, whereas liverworts, generally lacking these, grow flat along the ground.

Early Roots: the Liverwort

Since early plants lived on the shoreline of gigantic prehistoric oceans and in the swamps and bogs created by the receding water, the first roots probably helped more to hold a plant in place than to obtain food.

One plant that demonstrates this is the liverwort. Some varieties, although not all, show evidence of primitive roots, small hairs on the lower surfaces that serve to anchor the plant.

Amazing Mosses

Mosses improved on the idea. They provide clear evidence of having a primitive version of what has since become a stem. Branching hairs grow from these stems and those that contact the soil are incipient roots, functioning like modern, more complex versions.

Utilizing these elemental projections, mosses can absorb water and chemi-

LEFT: *The cycad* (Eurychone ssp.) *is a gymnosperm resembling the palm but reproducing by means of spermatozoids.* RIGHT: *Looking for all the world like trees, this is a close-up shot of moss.*

cals. They obtain nutrients not only from the soil but just as readily from rocks, decaying wood, and other surfaces.

Camel-like Mosses

While, as with any plant, they do require some water, many mosses are a plant-world equivalent of the camel: They can survive a surprisingly long time without it.

Even when they are virtually dried out, a little water brings them back to life.

World's First Flower?

No one knows which plant was the world's first flowering plant and certainly no one can be sure it has survived. But a good guess at one early pioneer is the cattail (*Typha latifolia*).

It has survived to the present time and gives us a picture of the distant past.

At first glance, it looks like a reed or rush. But it is actually a flowering plant—the only species in the genus.

Its flowers are tiny and extremely simple. The petals and sepals are represented by a few bristles, which make it look like a bottle-cleaner.

The flowers show signs of separate sexes and are placed one above the other on the same stem.

Flowering Plants

If we can believe fossil records, the first flowering plants probably appeared during the Jurassic, or second, period of the Mesozoic era.

Evidence comes from primitive pollen grains and flower fragments discovered in coal deposits in Scottish mines. Among the plants evolving then were ancestors of today's grains and forage grasses as well as palms, lilies, and orchids.

First Flowers

Not long ago scientists unearthed a surprising fossil, virtually a missing link, near Melbourne, Australia. The find was surprising because it established three factors not previously realized.

- First, the fossil was determined to be more than 120 million years old, five million years older than any previously known flower.
- Second, before this find, primitive flowers were considered to have been large and showy like the magnolia. This plant was barely one inch long.
- Third, it was seed-bearing and had a root system. Before this exciting find, experts were not certain that plants of that prehistoric age were capable of producing seeds or of having complex root systems.

It is possible that many of the world's thousands of seed-bearing plants are descendants of that small species. Gardeners would surely recognize similarities with today's wild yam, cat briar, and black pepper.

Horsetail

One primitive plant that has survived to our time is *Equisetum*, which means "horsetail." This plant can give you an excellent idea of what plant life was like in the Paleozoic era.

One element that points directly to its prehistoric past is its primitive root system, composed in part of a jointed hollow stem, very much like a straw for drinking.

The root is perennial. In the spring the cone-topped fruiting stems push their way upwards with surprising force. In modern times they've been known to lift large stones and break through well-tarred roads.

While there were more than 400 species at one time, the name seems odd when you realize that the plant came first: It has been in existence at least 100 million years longer than the horse.

A World Without Color

Flowers evolved in a time when the world was heavily forested. The trees were evergreens, cone-bearing trees called conifers, and animal life was dominated by such creatures as reptiles and beetles. There were no birds or butterflies.

It was a monotonous world, a planet without color or song. Yet somewhere on that prehistoric forest floor, the world's first flowers were developing.

Why did these flowers have no color? There was simply no reason for it. Beetles are practically color-blind and few reptiles had much interest in plants.

Why Are Flowers Colored?

The use of color is just one of the ways flowers attract pollinating insects. Early reproduction probably relied on the whims of the wind, just as plant life in the sea had relied on the water's changing patterns.

Then beetles began feeding on the sap and resin of those prehistoric

LEFT: *The cobra lily* (Darlingtonia californica) *is one of the most unusual plants in America. It is a carnivorous pitcher plant, one of nearly 200 varieties and species. They are mostly beautiful flowering plants with one difference—a trap to catch insects. The common assumption is that certain plants resort to trapping insects because amino acids are missing in their soil and this is how they make up for it.* RIGHT: *Horsetail* (Equisetum ssp.). *There are about 35 members in this extremely primitive family. Related to ferns, they propagate through the use of spores.*

evergreen cones. By returning regularly to feed on them, they accidentally carried male pollen to female plants and the pattern of insect pollination became established.

Beetle Flowers

The first flowers attracted beetles. Some examples still exist and today are most often found in the tropics. Since for beetles scent is more important than sight, color remains unimportant.

Early plants could attract these essential pollen-carriers by exuding smells a beetle could not pass up. Flowers that appeal to beetles generally have large, single blossoms. Examples include the magnolia and pond lilies.

Special Flowers for Special Insects

While some plants and trees continued to rely on the wind for pollination, as most flowers competed for insects to help with their reproduction, a large number began to specialize, appealing to specific creatures.

Today there are flowers that appeal to bees, others that appeal to moths, even some that attract flies, and still others that lure birds. A few flowers—perhaps the strangest of all—attract such oddities as snails.

Bee Flowers

Since bees like sweet and minty odors, and cannot see reds but are sensitive to such colors as yellow and violet, most flowers that attract bees are showy and extremely fragrant, and sport bright, light colors. All offer nectar. The list includes certain orchids, violets, verbena, blue columbine, larkspur, many snapdragons, and members of the mint and pea families. Many have a strong lower petal on which bees can land and most conceal their nectar inside, beyond the reach of other insects. Since bees fly only by day, bee flowers usually close at night.

The Bucket Orchid

Most flowers that attract bees simply lure them with nectar. However, the bucket orchid (*Coryanthes macrantha*) has a much more complex system, which unfolds something like a Hollywood movie.

The flower's fleshy lips are shaped like a bucket. Protrusions above them produce a heavily scented liquid, which seeps into the bucket. This liquid attracts male bees.

When bees land on the flower's lip, they immediately attempt to reach the source of the scent. They scratch at the flower, causing drops of the liquid to emerge—enough to make the bee drunk.

In a stupor, the intoxicated bee falls into the bucket. Slippery sides prevent his escape. Similar to an "Indiana Jones" movie, moments before the drunken bee drowns, he finds a narrow tunnel and wriggles through. The journey forces pollen from the orchid across his body.

But the poor fellow cannot be freed until he is sober, so nature has developed a trick: An obstruction on the top of the tunnel holds the bee for half an hour. Once released, the bee—now sober and alert—will find a second flower, repeating the performance. This time the bee will leave behind his cargo of precious pollen, enabling the orchid to produce seed.

Another Trick of Nature

Making visitors lose their footing seems to be a popular trick with several orchids. For instance, *Gongora grossa* has a lip as slippery as a banana peel. Any bee that lands on it is upended and slides on its back along a special curved column. As it slides, it picks up pollen. On the next involuntary ride, the bee deposits pollen on the flower's reproductive parts.

Varied Orchids

The orchid family illustrates an important point: Although flowers within a family are related, they may not look exactly alike, live the same way, or use the same pollinators. Differences such as these depend on many factors, including adaptations to local conditions.

Orchids utilize a variety of pollinators: bees, butterflies, and even hummingbirds.

In the tropics the bees that pollinate orchids are a solitary species. They do not live in hives and, like butterflies and moths, have a long tongue, which allows them to probe for nectar buried deep in the flower.

The Importance of Bees

Not every flower appeals to every species of bee. Nature has seen to it that each type of bee is suited to its own group of flowers.

While bees may not need flowers, many flowers could not survive without bees. In fact, without bees, an estimated 100,000 plant species would disappear from the earth.

Appealing to Bees

While most flowers attract bees by offering nectar, some attract them with pollen. A few, lacking either, attempt to attract bees with an enticement of fake sex.

For instance, an orchid of the genus *Ophrys* emits an odor that mimics the scent of a female bee. The plant even has a velvety surface that closely resembles that of the female bee.

Moth and Butterfly Flowers

Flowers that appeal to moths and butterflies also have special characteristics. Moths and butterflies can see reddish colors, so their flowers tend towards red and orange.

Nectar is an important lure, but since moths and butterflies do not rest on flowers as do bees, there is no need for a "landing platform." The petals on these flowers are small so that the moth or butterfly can hover close enough to reach the nectar.

There is a calculated match between the position of the nectar, which is found at the base of a long spur, and the length of the moth's or butterfly's tongue.

Madagascar Orchid

The Madagascar orchid (*Angraecum sesquipedale*), also known as the "Star-of-Bethlehem" because it blooms around Christmastime, has beautiful star-shaped, milk-white flowers, with waxy petals nearly half a foot across.

Its most surprising element, the feature that gave rise to its species name, is a long tube with nectar at the bottom.

Sesquipedale means "foot and one half," though the spur is commonly one foot deep.

When the great scientist Charles Darwin saw the plant, he predicted the existence of an insect able to probe for the deeply hidden nectar. Although most experts on insects laughed at the idea, an unusual moth was eventually found. It had a coiled tongue that, when straightened, measured exactly one foot in length.

This moth did seek out the orchid and did dine on its nectar.

Darwin's Book

Darwin was so enthralled by the unusual methods that orchids used to achieve pollination that he wrote a book with the long title *The Various Contrivances by Which Orchids Are Fertilized by Insects*.

Fly Flowers

At the other extreme are flowers that attract flies. A short tongue and a crude, unskilled approach are the prosaic characteristics of fly life. Nevertheless, fly flowers respond.

They do not specialize in nectar or sweet smells, but are dull in color and rank in smell—exactly what a fly wants.

One large-blossomed flower in Malaya lures flies with the odor of putrefying flesh. Another smells like dung. A Dutchman's-pipe (*Aristolochia*) smells like decaying vegetation.

Snail Flowers

Still other flowers are pollinated by gastropods, the ugly slugs and snails one finds in many gardens. To attract these, flowers often offer surprising rewards.

One member of the lily family, *Rohdea japonica*, offers a part of itself. Its fleshy flowers are half-hidden, attracting the gastropods with an unusual odor, which has been described as being like bad breath. As the snails dine on the petals, they also deposit pollen on the female stigma and, believe it or not, through the entire episode, the all-important female reproductive organ is never harmed.

The Plant That Lives Forever!

Although many prehistoric plants have become extinct, one common green alga is an exception. This plant does not reproduce by seeds or spores. Instead, it divides like a cell. You can truthfully say that the original green alga cell, which appeared millions of years ago, has never died. Some small part of it is still alive in millions of offspring.

The original plant divided to form two cells. Since that time, green algae cells have continued dividing and a minute part of the original cell plus bits from many of its earliest offspring can be found in the green algae living today.

Topsy-Turvy Time

At one time climates on Earth were very different. Colder countries were warm and sunny. Subtropical fruit, such as figs and breadfruit, thrived in Alaska and Greenland. But with the approaching Ice Age, climates stabilized and seasons, as we know them, developed.

The First Trees

Early trees were small, not much larger than some later flowers. In time they attained the size and form of those that we see today. Among them were certain of the softwood conifers that are around now.

Trees: Transformations

Some trees begin life looking like something else. The strangler fig comes into the world as a vine. Only with age does it come to resemble a tree.

One of a number of unusual plants seen in Australia, the *Xanthorrhoea* enters life looking like nothing more than a blade of grass.

As it grows, the leaves die and a bare stem tentatively rises skywards. In time the plant is topped with thick, greyish leaves, making it resemble an old man with a head of unruly hair.

A spike of flowers bursts from the middle and finally the blade of grass becomes a tree, standing 20 feet above the Australian desert.

The First Fruit Trees

At least three great tree species, two with descendants into our time, flourished during the Mesozoic era.

The ginkgo, or maidenhair, tree is one. Today it has the same finely veined, primitive-shaped leaves as its ancestors. It may have been the first tree to bear edible fruit. Its persimmonlike offering is edible, although not very tasty.

The Oldest Trees

Some of the world's oldest and largest trees grow in some of the coldest climates, the far north and in mountainous regions.

Early Trees

Gymnosperms, trees whose seeds develop without the essential female components, represent our most ancient trees. They date back more than 300 million years to the Carboniferous and Devonian periods. In that time vast forests covered the land and, while most species have long since become extinct, descendants of cone-bearers, such as pines and cedars, have managed to survive.

These are the trees that, along with ferns, have been used to create present-day coal and fossil fuels.

Largest Living Tree

The world's largest surviving tree, a giant sequoia (*Sequoiadendron*), is found at an elevation of 7,000 feet in California's Sierra Nevada mountains. Called the "General Sherman Tree," it is more than 3,500 years old and slightly more than 272.4 feet tall, nearly the length of a football field.

It measures more than 36 feet in diameter at its base and contains more than 50,010 cubic feet of wood, which means that "General Sherman" has the greatest bulk of any living thing.

Oldest Living Tree

The tree with the longest life span is a conifer, the bristlecone pine (*Pinus aristata*). It, too, is a western tree and, like the sequoia, can be found at very high elevations.

The oldest bristlecone pines are in California and Nevada.

The very oldest, a record-holder of more than 4,900 years of age, is found in the Wheeler Peak area of Nevada. It holds the record for longevity as the world's oldest living organism.

A bristlecone slightly younger, still judged to be more than 4,600 years of age, is found in the White Mountains of California.

The two trees are older than most of the world's civilizations. They were more than 1,000 years old when Buddha was born and were at least 2,000 years old when Christ preached at Galilee.

Northernmost Trees

While trees seem to grow older and taller in colder climates, they cannot survive everywhere. For example, there are no trees at the top of tall mountains.

The world's northernmost trees are those in a forest of black spruce (*Picea mariana*) in Alaska.

Tree-Sized Cactus

Tall trees do not exclusively inhabit cold climates and, in warmer areas, several other plants reach tree-sized proportions.

In the Galapagos Islands a cactus, *Jasminocereus*, reaches heights equal to many trees.

In regions of North America the saguaro cactus (*Cereus giganteus*) grows as high as 50 feet—taller than many trees. The biggest may weigh more than 10 tons.

Largest Cactus

The world's largest cactus is the cardon (*Pachycereus*). Found in parts of Mexico, it reaches heights of 60 feet.

This is the saguaro, a large treelike cactus.

Oldest Plant

The plant with the longest life span is the yucca (*Hesperoyucca*), a family of 40 species, including the familiar Spanish bayonet, Adam's needle, and the soap tree.

Some members can reach 30 feet in height and can live to be 200 to 300 years old.

First "Patented" Plant

On a sunny summer's day in 1938, George David Aiken, then both a professional horticulturist and governor of Vermont, discovered a particularly hardy and tasty wild strawberry plant. He dug it up and brought it back to a nursery in his home. After subdividing and caring for the plant for nine years, he announced the introduction of the Aiken "everbearing" strawberry. (The term indicates that the bush produces a late or bonus crop after its initial berries.)

This strawberry plant became the first variety of a commercial crop ever to receive a U.S. patent.

First Cultivated Plant?

The name of the first plant domesticated by man has been lost to history, but some paleobotanists, experts who look into such matters, believe that one strong possibility is the bottle gourd, the calabash *Lagenaria siceraria*. The name means "bottlelike drinking vessel" and, in early society, the gourd had both religious significance and considerable practical use.

On the religious side, it was thought to symbolize the beginning of the world and the creation of the human species. This symbolism was derived from its globelike shape and from the numerous seeds hidden inside.

On the practical side, it has been used for everything, from storage containers and drinking vessels to food, musical instruments, and even cricket and bird cages.

More than one expert has suggested that the gourd is responsible for agriculture. Early tribes possibly harvested it wild for its religious implications and then cultivated it for the same use. From that beginning evolved the vast agricultural society we know today.

First Garden Book

People have been writing about plants since before Christ, but most material dealt exclusively with their usefulness.

The first book to describe the pure joys of gardening was written in 1664. Despite its formidable title, *Kalendarium Hortense*, it was written by an English gardener, John Evelyn. Its sole purpose was to awaken people to the exciting world of plants and flowers.

2
WHAT'S IN A NAME?

Plant Names

Perhaps you've noticed that most plants have two types of name. The first is a *common name* such as daisy, marigold, aster, or pansy. Most of us use this when talking about plants. The second is a more formidable *botanical name*.

For example, one low-growing garden plant has the common name of dusty miller. It also has the botanical name of *Artemisia stellerana*.

In many instances, the botanical name *is* the common name. For example, a bougainvillea is known by that name around the world and, to a gardener, a coreopsis has only one name—coreopsis.

Common Names

Why two types of name? The problem is that common names are unreliable and confusing. Consider the daisy. Michaelmas and Shasta daisies seem related. They are not. A Michaelmas is really a hybrid aster (of *A novae-angliae* and *A novi-belgii*) and the Shasta is a member of the chrysanthemum family (*Chrysanthemum maximum*).

Botanist Liberty Hyde Bailey listed three distinct plants under the heading "flannel": flannelbush (*Fremontodendron*), flannel flower (*Actinotus helianthi*), and flannel plant (*Verbascum thapsus*). None of these plants have anything to do with each other.

There are at least six unrelated plants whose common name begins with "silver."

Over the centuries arum has accumulated more than a dozen common names. It has been known as jack-in-the-pulpit, skunk cabbage, lords-and-ladies, wake-robin, and more.

Consider the daffodil. The name is a corruption of "asphodel," which is a separate and distinctly different plant. The two are not related.

When the descriptive term "horse" appears in a common name, as it does in "horsetail" and "horse chestnut," it does not imply a resemblance to anything equestrian. In earlier times the word was simply a synonym for "crude."

Botanical Names

Botanical names are preferred over common names because they are usually more exact and the same words refer to the same plant the world over.

In general, the botanical name is composed of two words. The first describes the family or genus; the second names the specific type or species.

We utilize a similar concept with human names, although in the West we reverse it. "Robert Jones" means "Robert of the Jones family," exactly the information that plant names connote.

The Man Who Named Plants

The man who invented the system of botanical names used today was Charles, or Carolus, Linnaeus, a "Latinized" version of Carl von Linne.

His system, first published in 1737, was readily adopted around the world. Although it has been improved and modified, his basics are still in use.

Linne's real name was Nils Ingermarsson, but when he became a well-known botanist he took what he considered a more appropriate identification, choosing his last name from a giant linden tree that grew near his home.

Family, or Genus, Names

If you thought you could never speak a foreign language, it might be fun to realize that you do exactly that every time you use a botanical plant name. Most of the names have Latin or Greek roots, or have been "Latinized" with special endings.

The family, or genus, name indicates that the plant is related to a number of other plants with similar characteristics, usually apparent in their flowers, fruit, and leaves. Generally the family name ends in *aceae*.

For example, the family to which the violet belongs, called viola, has the botanical name *Violaceae*.

Species Names

Botanical names are commonly binomial, that is, composed of two terms.

The second, or species, name is called an epithet. It can be created in many

LEFT: *Shasta daisy* (Chrysanthemum x superbum), *a broadly cultivated plant, popular in gardens. This is a cultivated variety with more-than-normal-size blooms.* RIGHT: *Western thistle* (Cirsium occidentale) *is a member of the large* Compositae *family (carduus tribe). The botanical name is as direct as one can find.* Cirsium *is derived from the Greek* kirsion, *which means thistle.*

ways. It may be descriptive of some part of the plant or may be given as an honor or tribute. Many times it is the name of a person.

The Latinized ending of species names is usually either *ii* (pronounced eye) or *ana*.

The Latinized ending *ioideae* means "resembling" or "similar to."

Names That Honor

Consider the aster. The name of one, *Aster Tradescantii* (a garden flower popular in the eastern part of the United States), indicates that while the plant is a member of the aster family, the particular species has been selected to honor John Tradescant (1580–1638). The gentleman was a very well known naturalist and collector, and is regarded as the father of English gardening.

Berberis thunbergii, the Japanese barberry, is another example. Berberis is the Latinized version of the Arabic name for the plant, berber. *Thunbergii* comes from Thunberg. Carl P. Thunberg (1743–1828) was a botanist-explorer who collected plants in the Orient. He made a number of important discoveries and Linnaeus acknowledged his services by naming this plant in his honor.

The popular shrub weigela was named for a well-known Swiss botanist, C. E. Weigel (1748–1831).

Darwinia, the evergreen scented myrtle, honors Charles Darwin.

LEFT: *Evening primrose* (Oenothera hookeri). *Varieties of the primrose family cover the globe. Some are low and weedy; others have larger, showier flowers. This one, named for the famous botanist Joseph Hooker, is rare and is found on California's Channel Islands.* RIGHT: *Related to the evening primrose,* Clarkia amoena *is a beautiful wildflower, with a number of common names, including last-of-spring and summer's darling. The flower's genus name honors Captain William Clark, of the Lewis and Clark expedition, who crossed the Rocky Mountains in 1806, returning with a large botanical sampling, including this. The evening primrose family,* Onogracaea, *is represented by a number of western wildflowers. Perhaps the best known is the fuchsia.*

Plants Named for Gods and Legends

Some plants were named for Greek gods and goddesses. For instance, the iris was named for the goddess of the rainbow. The hyacinth was named for an unfortunate youth who was accidentally slain by the god Apollo.

The crown imperial (*Fritillaria imperialis*) was named for an early Christian legend. The flower is said to have stared boldly at Christ on His way to His Crucifixion and, so shamed by its action, the plant has hung its head ever since.

Behind Botanical Names

If you could peek behind the often imposing Latin or Greek botanical names, you would find that they are generally more direct and descriptive than you might have suspected. What follows are the meanings of some botanical names. Many were created by Carolus Linnaeus himself and describe some special attribute of the plant.

Artichoke, Globe, *Cynara scolymus*

The first name is a Latinized version of *Kunos*, a form of the Greek word for dog. It is descriptive of the "guard" leaves that surround the flower. Botanists thought that these leaves resembled dog teeth.

Scolymus comes to us straight from Latin and means artichoke.

Asparagus, *Asparagus officinalis*

The name is Latin, derived from the Greek word *asparagos*. It means a sprout or shoot. Botanists thought the term described the plant perfectly.

Whenever you see *officinalis* as the second botanical name, it indicates that the species had a culinary or medicinal use and was a commercial or "crop" plant.

Astilbe, *Astilbe simplicifolia*

The Green word *astilbe* means "not shining." It was probably selected for its reference to the dullish, unremarkable leaves that are characteristic of the plant.

Simplicifolia means "simple-leaved." The term was chosen to call attention to the leaf design. It is undivided and lacks complexity.

Avocado, *Persea Americana*

There is a story behind all three names.

Avocado is derived from the original Aztec name for the fruit, *ahaucotl*. In Aztec, the word meant "testicle tree," a terse reference to the shape of the fruit. When translated into Spanish, the name became *aquacate*. Eventually it got corrupted into the name we use today.

The botanical names indicate confusion by early scientists and a later attempt to correct the mistake.

Persea was chosen because early botanists were under the impression that the fruit came from Persia.

Americana was added later in an attempt to show where the plant really originated.

Baby's Breath, *Gypsophila repens*

Here, the first word, *Gypsophila*, means "chalk-loving" and tells botanists the type of soil the plant prefers—chalky.

The second word, *repens*, means "creeping" and indicates the way the plant grows.

Balsam, Sweet, *Melissa officinalis*

In Greek, *Melissa* means honeybee. The name was selected to indicate the bee's great love for the flower.

Again, *officinalis* shows that the plant had a medicinal or food use at the time it was named.

Beard Tongue, *Pentstemon digitalis*

The first word, *Pentstemon*, from the Greek, refers to the plant's five stamens. Four are always active; the fifth is sterile.

Digitalis, a Latin word, means "in the form of fingers," again referring to the stamens.

The common name, beard tongue, arose from the fifth or sterile stamen having a bearded-tongue–like appearance. For some reason, the paradox took the botanist's fancy.

Buttercup Family, *Ranunculus spp.*

Within this family, there are 50 herbs and shrubs and some 1,900 species. In Latin, *Ranunculus* means "froglike."

Chinese Hat or Cup-and-Saucer, *Holmskioidia sanguinea*

The plant was named in honor of Theodor Holmskjold (1732–1794)—hence, the first word. Holmskjold was a Danish nobleman and botanist.

The second word refers to the blood-red flowers. The plant is a spiny shrub from India.

Chrysanthemum

This name is actually from two Greek words, *chrysos* and *anthemon*, meaning "golden flower." Chrysanthemums are popular the world over.

Coriander, *Coriandrum sativum*

In Greek *Coriandrum* means "bug." The name was chosen because botanists thought the plant had an insectlike odor.

Sativum means "sown as a crop," an indicator that the plant has long been domesticated and commercially grown.

Garden Heliotrope, *Valeriana officinalis*

From the Latin *valere*, the name means strong and healthy, a reference to the hardiness of the plant.

Heartleaf Philodendron, *Philodendron cordatum*

Long before it was domesticated, the plant was a tree-climber. The word *Philodendron* tells us that. In Greek it means "tree-loving."

A Latin word, *cordatum* refers to the heart-shaped leaves.

Pot Marigold, *Calendula officinalis*

This plant was given its botanical name because it blooms throughout the months. In Latin *calendae* means "the first day of the month." When dried, its flowers were thought to cure warts.

Rue

Rue is an herb with bitter-tasting leaves. This common name was given as a reminder that one would rue it, or regret it, if one took even one taste. Rue is derived from the Greek word *rhytē*.

Scaly Bromeliad, *Aechmea pubescens*

This is a popular, tree-growing bromeliad. *Aechmea* is derived from the Greek word *aichme*, which means "spear tip." It refers to the shape of the leaves.

The second word, *pubescens*, from Latin, means "covered with powdery scales," which also describes the plant.

Smoke Tree, *Dalea spinosa*

Common in the deserts of western America, this plant received its botanical name because once its small leaves are shed, they reveal a network of grey, spiny branches.

The branches also have a "smokey" appearance, which accounts for the common name.

Sunflower, *Helianthus*

The sunflower got its name because the open face of the flower resembles the sun and because, during the day, it follows the sun's path. In Greek mythology, *Helios* was the sun, one of the twelve great gods of Olympus.

Yam, *Dioscorea batatas*

The first name was chosen to honor Pendanius Dioscorides, the first-century (A.D.) author of the five-volume *De Materia Medica*, one of the first books to discuss the medicinal uses of herbs.

The species word, *batatas*, means "potatoes" and indicates that the plant is an edible tuber. The word is the predecessor of our own word "potatoes."

The common name, yam, comes from the African word *nyami*, which means "to eat."

Religious Meanings

Through man's long and traditional connection with nature, much of nature has acquired special associations, most of them religious. For instance, in China, as in the Old and New Testaments, the gourd has special meaning. What follows are some of the most common and most interesting symbolizations.

Acacia

A group of more than 800 shrubs and trees, the acacia has particular significance in the Jewish religion.

The Ark of the Covenant was made from the wood of one variety of acacia tree.

There are frequent biblical references to "shittim" wood. When this term is used, it refers to the shittah tree, an ancient Middle Eastern acacia.

Many religious scholars believe this was also the burning bush from which God spoke to Moses.

Aloe *(Aloe succotrina)*

This plant has been known for centuries in Egypt, Israel, and other Middle Eastern countries. The sap or juice extracted from it was used in embalming and purifying the dead.

When it came time to bury Jesus, Nicodemus offered a costly mixture of myrrh and aloe.

Anemone

The variety of lilies that Westerners often associate with Easter are rare in Palestine. Thus, biblical references to "lilies of the field" have been taken to mean some other flower. Amaryllis and violets are among those suggested, but many experts believe that the simple anemone is the best guess of all.

Today's American gardener has a choice of some 120 species.

Anthurium

On Luther's coat of arms, the flower symbolized the heart. Anthurium is a shade-loving plant and some species produce extremely beautiful blooms.

Aspalathus

The Lord's wisdom was likened to this sweet-smelling, shrubby member of the pea family.

Bean, Black and White

Beans were used in voting. A white bean signified a "yes" vote; a black bean signified a "no."

Boxwood *(Buxus)*

This tree signifies a period of continuous grace and prosperity for the Church.

Isaiah 41:19—"I will set in the desert the fir tree, the pine and the box together that they may see . . . that the hand of the Lord hath done this. . . ."

Carnation

Early German poets considered it a symbol of and a tribute to the Virgin Mary.

Cedar

A number are mentioned.

Psalms 91:12—"The righteous . . . shall grow like a cedar in Lebanon." The reference is to *Cedrus libani*.

C. deodara, the most durable of the cedars and a native of the Himalayas, is the species that has been selected to symbolize incorruptible faith and a steadfast, unchanging view.

Chinese Evergreen

A symbol of long life.

Chrysanthemum

Another symbol of long life.

Columbine

This plant has two meanings. First, since *columba* in Latin means "dove," this has become the flower of the dove. It is also considered the sacred symbol of the Holy Ghost, who is usually represented as as dove.

Crocus

Much praised in the Song of Songs.

Cypress *(Cupressus sempervirens,* "Italian Cypress")

Since the earliest times, this tree has been a symbol of mourning. In some instances, it has also been considered a sign of immortality.

Dianthus

Represents divine love.

Dogwood

According to some legends, this was the tree on which Christ was crucified. As the story goes, the tree pitied the Lord's suffering and, as a reward, Christ promised that it would never again grow large enough to be used in that manner.

The blossoms form a cross, which is also seen as a symbol of the Crucifixion.

Fig

An early biblical fruit, it is sometimes used to symbolize lust.

LEFT: *Dogwood* (Cornus ssp.). *Noted for its spectacular early bloom, the dogwood is one of the few trees that blooms before its leaves appear. As far as trees go, it is small. In legend, the tree was used for Christ's cross at Calvary and was promised that it would never again grow large enough to be used for such an evil purpose.* RIGHT: *Bush lupin* (Lupinus ssp.). *The genus name comes from the Latin* lupus, *meaning "wolf," because early botanists thought the plant robbed the soil of essential nutrition. Actually, the plant, which is a member of the pea family (thus, a legume), benefits the soil through the presence of helpful bacteria housed in its nodules. These recover nitrogen from the air and turn it into compounds that fertilize the soil.*

Gardenia

Chastity and femininity.

Gladiolus

Represents abundance, generosity, and the Incarnation, that is, the taking on of human form by Jesus. In Hebrew it is called *sushan*.

Gourd

Long an important symbolic plant, a gourd can signify creation, death, and resurrection. In China the seeds represent the "ten thousand things," which is to say, the uncounted real world.

Grape

Sometimes specifically named and sometimes referred to obliquely as "the vine," the grape has several important meanings.

As used in the Eucharist, grape wine is believed to represent—or to actually become—the blood of Christ.

Twelve bunches represent the twelve apostles.

In literature the clusters can also symbolize revelry.

Holly

Bramble, in biblical terminology, generally means any thorny plant. A local species may be the plant that was used to make Jesus's Crown of Thorns.

If one species must be named, many biblical experts think the original reference was to *Rubus ulmifolius*, which doesn't really make sense since the species is thornless. Others suspect *R. coronarius*, the brier rose, or *R. dumetorum*, European dewberry.

Hyssop

Freshness and cleanliness.

Ivy

Fidelity and eternity.

Jasmine

Occasionally associated with the Virgin Mary.

Juniper

In the Bible, it is mentioned as the "Algum" tree.

Laurel

Both the sweet and bay laurel can represent eternity and triumph.

Lily

The Easter lily (*Lilium longiflorum*) represents life and resurrection.
The scarlet lily (*L. chalcedonicum*) is mentioned in the Song of Songs.
The Madonna lily was named to honor the Virgin Mary.

Lotus *(Nymphae, or Nelumbo)*

One of the world's first sacred plants, it was revered by the Egyptians and is
extremely important in Buddhism.

*The lotus (genus, Nymphaea) and the common water lily (genus, Nelumbo), in the Guilder-
son Japanese gardens at the University of California at Los Angeles.*

1: Hundreds of wildflowers such as these daisylike blooms are members of the Compositae *family, the largest genus of garden flowers. 2: Indian onion, or wild onion, (Allium lacunosum). More than 500 species of wild onion are found in the Northern Hemisphere. 3: Typical Alaskan summer scenery. Meadow and tundra areas are often flowered with lupin, angelica, and false hellebore. 4:* Heracleum lanatum, *cow parsnip, also known as wild celery, Indian celery, and hogweed. Named for Hercules, the plant can reach heights of 6 to 9 feet.*

A

1: *The tulip—variety, Appledorn. Tulip bulbs have been eaten as food for centuries, and, in Crete, one variety is regarded as a springtime delicacy.* 2: Pieris tiawanensis, *an evergreen shrub, also known as lily-of-the-valley-bush, is popular for bonsai plantings.* 3: *Camellia, from the* Theacea *family. The genus is best known for the leaves of* Camellia sinensis, *the tea plant.* 4: *The primrose, from the* Primula *genus, a large one with 400 species.* 5: *The cobra lily* (Darlingtonia californica) *is a carnivorous pitcher plant that traps and digests insects.*

B

1: A field of wild mustard and blooming fruit trees. Mustard is made from the seeds of several varieties and has been used as a condiment since early times. 2: The English daisy (Bellis perennis), a member of the Compositae family. 3: Iris—variety, violet. The designs on the inner flower parts attract insects and direct them to the pollen. 4: The greatest display of cactus can be found in the Mexican desert. 5: Aspen and birch, in a forest in Utah. The genus Populus also includes poplar and cottonwood.

C

1: Purple Azalea. The name is derived from the Greek azaleos, meaning "dry." The plant was so named because it was supposed to grow best in dry ground. 2: Some of the showier cabbages, like the rumpled-leaved savoy pictured here, are planted as ornamentals. 3: The California poppy (Eschscholzia californica), from the papaver family. Opium is derived from only one variety, P. somniferum. 4: The Gaillardia, another member of the Compositae family. These plants are great for cut flowers but, being annual, must be reseeded.

D

LEFT: *Marguerite, generally considered a member of the aster tribe (genus* Compositae), *illustrates the problem of common names. The common white marguerite is* Chrysanthemum frutescens. *When it is blue, it is a member of the genus* Felicia *and, when it is golden yellow, it is most often of the genus* Anthemis. *Confusing? Just enjoy it by its common name.* RIGHT: *Magnolia blossoms. The magnolia is one of nature's most primitive and earliest flowering trees.*

Magnolia

Chinese legend proclaims it as one of the three most loved plants. In the West, it stands for power and pride.

Mustard Seed

Implies steadfast faith with a touch of much needed patience, as in "A mustard seed can move a mountain."

Myrtle

Popular in pre-Christian Greece. Myrtle wreaths were presented to winners in many sports competitions.

Oleander

Said to represent danger because its leaves are extremely poisonous.

Olive

The olive branch was a common symbol of peace long before Christian times. It was the branch brought by a dove to Noah as a sign of "land ahead" after the Deluge.

What's in a Name? 33

Orange

The orange is one of our first domesticated fruits. Its global shape is seen to represent the world.

Palm

Victory and eternal peace. In Greece and early Rome, palm leaves were given to winners in contests of skill and strength.

Pansy

Remembrance.

Passionflower *(Passiflora)*

The plant symbolizes Christ's suffering. Each part has special significance. The 10 petals represent the apostles who did not deny or betray the Lord. The five stamens are equated with the five wounds of Jesus. The three styles stand for the nails through His hands and feet. The flower's ray signifies the Crown of Thorns. The tendrils symbolize the cords with which the Lord was bound, and the leaves remind one of the spears used by Roman guards.

Peach Blossom

Long life.

Pear

The shape reminds many of the human heart.

Pine

Faithfulness. In China it is highly revered as a symbol of lasting support and is associated with the crane, an honored and protected bird.

Pomegranate

Its many seeds symbolize fertility. The flower represents immortality and hope.

Pussy Willow

Especially meaningful in England where, on Palm Sunday, sprigs are given to young Sunday school students.

Rose

Symbolizes the promised Messiah. A red rose represents love and martyrdom; a white rose symbolizes purity. It is the official flower of Father's Day.

Shamrock

The Holy Trinity.

Strawberry

Good works and righteousness.

Wheat

Represents the bounty of the earth, the "staff of life." Baked, it becomes the bread of the Eucharist, the body of Christ.

Willow

In early times it was thought to symbolize the Holy Gospel, because no matter how badly treated or bent, it does not break, and even when numerous branches are cut, it remains alive and vibrant.

Yew

Symbolizes immortality, rest, and occasionally sorrow. In the Old Testament, it was seen as providing a place for rest and meditation when one was troubled.

Commonly Used Plant Terms

Terms describing the parts of plants and flowers belong to a world of their own. What follows are definitions for these words along with definitions for some other terms commonly used by botanists and gardeners.

Achene: a small, seedlike fruit, featuring a single seed.

Anther: the upper part of the stamen, that segment containing pollen.

Axil: the angle created by two parts of a flower, the upper side of a leaf and the stem from which it rises.

Basal leaves: those seen at the base of a stem.

Bipinnate leaf: a complex leaf, generally divided into secondary components.

Bracts: modified leaf forms, commonly situated at the base of a flower.

Campanulate: shaped like a bell.

Composite flower: a cluster of smaller flowers that are grouped to form, or give the appearance of, a larger flower.

Cordate: shaped like a heart.

Corolla: together, the petals of one flower.

Corymb: a type of cluster in which the lower stems are longest (see also **Inflorescence**).

Dioecious: a species or type in which male and female flowers are carried on separate plants.

Exserted: (a part) extending beyond, i.e., stamens that protrude beyond a corolla.

Fimbriate: with a fringe.

Glabrous: bald

Glaucous: a powdery substance on leaf surfaces, generally white.

Inflorescence: the arrangement of clustered flowers.

Lanceolate leaf: shaped like a lance.

Monoecious: containing male and female flowers on the same plant.

Node: the point on a stem where branches or leaves attach.

Oblanceolate leaf: shaped like the head of a lance.

Obovate leaf: shaped like an egg, with the narrowest point at the base.

Ovate leaf: shaped like an egg, with the broadest point at the base.

Palmate: shaped like the fingers of a hand, with at least three divisions.

Peduncle: a flower's stem or stalk when inflorescence consists of a single flower.

Petiole: the part of a leaf that attaches to a stem, generally stalklike.

Pistil: the female component of a flower, composed of a visible stigma, a tubular style, and an ovary, commonly at the base.

Pollen: the male component that, when lodged in the ovary, produces seed. Commonly found in the anther.

Pubescent: covered with hair or scales.

Reniform: kidney-shaped.

Rhizome: an underground stem, normally horizontal, modified as a food-storage component.

Sagittate: shaped like an arrowhead.

Sessile: minus a stalk.

Spatulate leaf: a leaf with a broad, rounded end and a narrow base; a leaf shaped like a spatula.

Stigma: the tip of the pistil—that portion that receives the male pollen.

Succulent: a plant with fleshy, water-storing leaves—cactus, for example.

Undulate: with a wavy outer edge.

Whorled: circular, with leaves—generally three or more.

3
ROOTS AND SOIL

Taking Root

Most of us would describe a root as the portion of a plant that functions beneath the ground. Many roots do just that. They anchor the plant, support the portion that grows above, absorb moisture, and gather and/or store nourishment.

But not all plants have roots and not all roots grow underground.

Strange Roots

Some roots, such as those attached to a plant known as "frog's bit" (*Hydrocharis*), live entirely in water.

The roots of some orchids function much like leaves. The species *Angraecum* is one example. Its roots grow entirely in the air.

On parasitic plants—that is, those that survive through the work of others—the roots rarely, if ever, touch ground. For example, mistletoe (*Phoradendron*) lives by penetrating the sap stream of trees. Its roots are connected to the ground, which can be 40 feet below, only through intermediaries.

Spanish moss (*Tillandsia usneoides*), a strange relative of the pineapple family and neither a moss nor Spanish, lives above ground. Conceivably, the plant would be able to face the day as happily on a fence post as on a tree branch, since it spends its entire life without true roots.

Hardworking Roots

For many plants—those that possess true roots—the section beneath the earth is more extensive than the portion above ground.

Some grasses, showing an inch or two of growth above the surface, may have roots that penetrate as deep as 13 feet.

An alfalfa plant, which might reach modest above-ground heights, can have an underground root system as long as 30 feet.

In one season, the root system of a corn plant may penetrate as deep as 8 feet.

No Rest for Roots

While the above-ground portion of a plant may take an occasional rest, shedding leaves for a winter's nap, the roots of perennials work year-round. In winter, they expand, enter new territory, and—even with snows piled high above ground—must prepare for the approaching spring.

When the dormancy ends, it is the roots that must energize the buds and sustain the production of new leaves until they are large enough to function on their own.

Importance of Light

Even though roots live underground, most are affected by light. Sunlight, whether or not it reaches roots directly, is a source of power for them. It affects their metabolism and their ability to work.

Root Sense

Roots can sense both direction and approaching problems.

Reverse a seed and a plant still grows normally—root system down, stem up.

Confronted by a small rock, roots sense the obstruction and grow around it.

Confronting something more formidable, a root will slow its growth to avoid impact.

Often it will cope by changing direction and, if there is no other way around, another part of the root system will take over.

Confronted by sterile clay, a few roots may test the soil while other roots try a new course, seeking richer, more beneficial territory.

Roots Take Control

Roots seem to control many of the things a plant does. For example, roots are a major decision-maker when it comes to dormancy, the time when a plant ceases to produce and enters a period of "rest." Shedding of leaves, one indicator of approaching dormancy, occurs in many plants and trees. It begins when the roots send a special substance to the base of each leaf.

This substance creates a unique "weak link" between the leaf and the stalk. Once the process is completed, the leaf drops.

The Importance of Water

From the time a seed germinates, water is indispensable. Every part of a growing plant needs a share so that it can function. Roots are no exception.

A portion of the water absorbed by roots is used for their own chemical activities.

Some helps to cool, or "air-condition," the root system.

Liquid also helps roots to hold their shape. Water pressure from within counterbalances outside pressures from the soil, keeping roots intact.

Generous quantities of water are required to carry the large amount of nutrients collected from the soil.

Root Pressures

The pressures of liquids within a root vary with the plant. They are low in shade trees and high in many vines.

Remove a leaf from a grapevine, especially in the spring, and sap may squirt from the opening, like water from a cracked pipe. Yet, in a pine tree, pressure is so slight that it cannot be measured with normal instruments.

Those drops of moisture that sparkle so invitingly on blades of grass each morning may not have come from above. Chances are they represent surplus moisture pushed through the plant system from below ground.

A low-growing sun rose can generate this many roots in a small container. Consider what it could do in soil.

The Soil: Common Ground

Roots, the essential footing that holds a plant in place and collects moisture and nutrition for survival and growth, share the soil with millions of neighbors—specifically, bacteria, fungi, and insects.

Many are so small that man has yet to count them. Some are friendly, while others are deadly enemies. Some are dependent on roots, whereas others maintain a cooperative relationship.

Plant Diseases

Like humans, plants are susceptible to numerous diseases. Underground, disease-carrying bacteria, unfriendly insects such as nematodes, and dangerous larvae add up to a serious problem. No one knows exactly how many diseases affecting plants exist, but some reliable pathologists maintain there are as many as 700,000. This number may be outrageously high.

On a more conservative note, experts at the U.S. Department of Agriculture currently list more than 120,000, and are still counting.

Nasty Nematodes

The nematode, or threadworm, is both dangerous and remarkable.

Lacking a developed brain, it has been outsmarting man for centuries.

Minus a nose, it can trail its quarry as closely as a bloodhound.

It has survived longer than man and is ubiquitous, found almost from pole to pole.

The threadworm list includes some of the most ruthless pests of roots as well as parasites harmful to fish, birds, and mammals including man.

The largest, sometimes 20 feet in length, is a seagoing threadworm most often found infesting whales.

No fewer than 30 smaller species cause human diseases, including anemia and trichinosis.

Many attack roots. The tobacco plant was among the first. Other victims include tomato, potato, and okra.

On the plus side, there are many beneficial nematodes, which are actually helpful to gardeners. They improve plant life by attacking those species that damage crops.

Important Topsoil

Most of today's root pathogens, bacteria and other culprits injurious to roots, live in the upper reaches of the soil.

Many can be found no deeper than the first 6 inches.

Most of the nutrients, moisture, and beneficial bacteria and fungi also inhabit that narrow stratum of topsoil. Like Times Square at noon, it is a busy area.

One expert insists that 60 percent of all soil-borne diseases can be found in the first 3-inch stratum. Most agree that 90 percent of all enemies of roots live in the first foot of soil.

Roots Make Decisions

What happens if you graft the above-the-ground segment of a young tomato plant to the roots of a tobacco plant?

The experiment proves that roots control a plant's future, literally deciding what kind of a plant the top part will become.

The above-ground part of the plant will continue to look exactly like a tomato plant, but there will be chemical changes.

The leaves may signal "tomato," but their chemical content will have been altered. Now, they will exude an almost colorless alkaloid, known as nicotine.

Processed as tobacco, the leaf can be chewed or smoked, is guaranteed to stain teeth, and could probably odorize the breath as quickly as any conventional tobacco plant.

Other Roots

While roots are generally formed from special parts of a plant beneath the ground, some segments above ground are able to produce roots as well.

In a process called "layering," when a branch of certain plants touches ground, a root begins to form, creating, in time, a new plant.

In special cases, this can occur some distance above ground in the air. The process is called "air layering."

An Australian Example

One strange tree that grows on the windswept islands of the South Pacific manages to survive by "layering." High winds blowing across the sandy islands of the Great Barrier Reef in outer Australia often topple even the sturdiest of trees.

Through an unusual system of rooting, *Pisona grandis* has managed to survive, even though the tree is blown over time and time again.

Its survival technique is simple. When the tree is uprooted, it literally reaches out with any convenient branch, makes new roots, and continues growing.

LEFT: *The root of the taro plant has been eaten by mankind for centuries. It was probably one of the first to be harvested. There are two species:* Alocasia macrorrhiza *and* Colocasia esculenta. Colocasia *is the best known, grown widely for food and as an ornamental plant. Usually known by its common name, elephant's ear, it is regularly used as food in Hawaii and on many Pacific islands.* RIGHT: *Shield fern* (Polystichum dudleyi). *Ferns are flowerless plants, generally primitive in nature, producing true roots from a rhizome. About 120 species of shield fern have been described. Varieties can be found in Europe as well as America. The variety here,* dudleyi, *is common in California and as far north as Alaska.*

Chemical Warfare: How Plants Handle Competition

Trouble often arises when two plants compete for resources. Animals drive off competition directly, but plants must use a more subtle approach.

One trick is *antibiosis*, a method by which one plant deters another through the use of chemicals, a kind of underground warfare. It is a trick that plants have used for centuries.

The premise is the same as that behind man's use of such antibiotics as *Penicillium*. If you remember, the mould secretes a substance that prevents the growth of competing organisms. That is the reason doctors use it.

In the same vein, one common grass, *Aristida oligantha*, secretes phenolic acid. The acid inhibits the development of bacteria that create nitrogen in the soil. A lack of nitrogen slows the approach of competition.

Seeds such as the common shepherd's purse (*Capsella bursapastoris*) are protected by a special secretion. The compound can attract, kill, and even digest many underground pests, including mosquito larvae, nematodes, and destructive bacteria.

Surprising Parasites

Nature's versatility is exemplified in the numerous species of one South American plant. Most of them are parasites of one kind or another and live happily well above ground.

While plants generally become parasites because they can no longer manufacture their own food, a plant with the tongue-stumbling name of *Phrygilanthus mutabilis* is both an evergreen and a parasite, which means that the plant could make its own food if it wanted to.

Because of competition or for other reasons, it has chosen to become a parasite, taking food produced by the southern beech—stealing might be a more accurate word.

P. mutabilis finds a comfortable home on a beech branch, burrows into the tree's sap line, and lives, without any work of its own, on the tree's processed sugars.

Another species attacks a South American tree cactus, *Ceres chilensis*, and in the process the two literally become one.

The parasite even lets the cactus bear its flowers. In time, red flowers typical of the parasite erupt from the cactus, just as if they were flowers of the cactus, which they are not.

Carbon Dioxide and Growth

Oxygen and carbon dioxide are important elements in plant growth. Plants produce about 20 percent of the required CO_2 from the soil. The rest must be obtained from the air around them. Thus, 80 percent of the essential CO_2 must be "blown in" from surrounding areas.

This is one reason why, on quiet and windless days, plants may show less growth.

In addition, maximum access to CO_2 increases a plant's ability to absorb moisture.

For a gardener, this means that rows of shrubs and bushes that could block the flow of air to neighboring plants can directly affect the health and growth rate of shorter plants situated behind them.

Miracle Chemical

One "energy" chemical supplied by the roots and used by leaves is ATP (adenosine triphosphate). This essential, high-energy chemical helps produce necessary amino acids and proteins.

If you consider leaves as the "engines" that produce the power to keep plants alive, you can say that ATP is the chemical that "jump-starts" the engines.

Dangerous Soil Minerals

Sometimes plants are endangered by minerals lifted to the roots by deep plowing.

Aluminum is a major offender. It presents little danger in low-acid soils (the metal remains insoluble), but, in acid soils, the presence of aluminum can be harmful. It's especially dangerous to such plants as cotton. The toxicity can affect tender root cells. In many areas, manganese presents a similar danger.

Plant Friends and Enemies

Early Greek writers realized that certain plants grew well together while others had problems relating.

The Roman scholar Pliny the Elder (Gaius Plinus Secundus) (23–79 A.D.) insisted that rue and basil hated each other and added that the radish was an enemy of the perennial herb, hyssop.

It has been only in recent years that experts have discovered that there is some truth behind such claims.

Certain crops *do* thrive beside friendly neighbors, while others cannot even follow one another in the same field.

Corn and soybeans are the best of friends. When grown together, the increased nitrogen supplied by the soybean roots helps farmers grow some of the healthiest, largest corn found anywhere.

On the other hand, corn is most unhappy if planted close to sugar beets.

It does not do well even when planted later in a field that previously held sugar beets. The reason: a lack of zinc, a minor, yet obviously important, mineral.

It seems that sugar-beet roots create changes in soluble zinc, rendering it less available to subsequent crops.

Unique Teamwork

You could call it the *mycorrhizal* connection, a unique cooperative action between the roots of some higher plants and certain fungi.

Fungi can derive nourishment from the decaying matter around them, while higher plants cannot.

Because of potential dietary deficiencies, some plants, such as conifers and beech trees and certain orchids, have an arrangement through which fungi absorb nourishment from decaying matter and pass it along to them. Otherwise, they would not be able to utilize it.

4

MARVELS OF
REPRODUCTION

Pure Plants

In early times flowers were thought to be nature's prime example of purity. It was thought that they were so ethereal that the various species reproduced without help, rising spontaneously from the soil that held them.

When an English doctor, Sir Thomas Millington, suggested otherwise in 1676, he was nearly driven from London.

The Real Secret

Flowers, those bright and shining orbs we see in gardens, have been created for just one purpose: to guarantee the future of the species.

The bottom line is pragmatic, not aesthetic. The blooms are attractive because they are reproductive organs brightened and colored to appeal to insects, birds, and other creatures.

On some plants, they are exclusively male. On others, they are female. In still other cases, male and female elements are combined on a single plant or in a single flower.

Plant-World Reproduction

Plants have reproductive components that function in a similar manner to those of humans. On the male side, the organs consist of a slender stalk called a *stamen* (from the Greek word meaning "hair or thread") and a rounded *anther* on which pollen is displayed.

For the female element, the *pistil* in the middle of a flower includes the *style*, a stalklike tube, and the *stigma*, a rounded segment that rises from it. The *ovary*, in which seed is produced, is usually not visible. Most often it is hidden deeper in the flower.

Nature's First Sex Life

Experts suggest that the span of time between the first appearance of life in the waters of our planet and the point at which it could reproduce through some process resembling sex was something on the order of two billion years.

During that vast span of time, the life process itself improved, with primitive forms becoming increasingly more complex.

Prior to reaching a necessary state of complexity, life forms were literally too crude for sex.

Pollinators

Plant reproduction is generally accomplished through the use of spores and pollen. Since plants are rooted and immobile, they are forced to rely on "messengers," outsiders recruited to carry the male pollen to female plants.

Some species rely on a single insect; others attract a carefully limited number. Still others welcome any and all visitors.

When flowers rely on a single insect for pollination, they are said to be "insect specific." In this case, their component parts are usually carefully designed to accommodate the visiting insect.

There are more than 150 species of penstemon, a bright-faced flower found in the countryside as well as in gardens. Two varieties of penstemon can serve as examples.

One variety with narrow, tubular flowers, *P. centranthifolius*, is irresistible to hummingbirds. Not only are hummingbirds drawn by the color of its brilliant carmine flowers, but the flowers themselves seem designed for the little visitors. Nectar is hidden at the bottom of a tube just long enough for the bird's slender beak and the bottom petal is flat so that the birds can hover close in without restriction.

Another variety, *P. palmeri*, is attractive to bees. Its creamy-white flowers offer everything a bee might want: a wide throat, an unobstructed mouth, and a lower petal sturdy enough to support a bee as it lands.

Importance of Pollen

Male pollen is one of two essentials needed to produce new plants. The other is the female element found in the ovary.

The role of pollen in producing fruit and new plants has been known for centuries.

Thousands of years before Christ, the world's earliest growers, the Assyrians and the Egyptians, hung branches of male palm flowers in female trees to be certain of fruit.

From Spores to Pollen

It is generally agreed that minute, almost invisible spores were employed in nature's first method of reproduction. It was a system used by the more primitive land-based plants.

Such terrestrial insects as beetles discovered the spores and included them in their diet. The movement of insects from plant to plant in search of spores brought about the process of "pollination" and, when spores evolved into today's pollen, the procedure continued.

For millions of years, pollen was the main ingredient that attracted insects.

Finally color and nectar were added. Not only do both help to entice many more insects, but they also make the procedure more efficient.

As life evolved, more sophisticated attractants were added.

An Ideal Food

Many insects, bees and others, are attracted by pollen. It is an ideal food and many insects collect it, generally to feed their young.

Pollen is especially rich in protein (up to thirty percent) and low in calories (as it is one-to-seven-percent starch, one-to-ten-percent sugars, and about five-percent fat).

Unique Pollen Cells

Pollen is protected by one of the world's most durable packages, a double shell made up of a tough, resistant outer cover and a porous yet sturdy inner one.

The outer surface of the shell is decorated with a special pattern that, like a fingerprint, is unique to the species. No two plant varieties have the same pattern.

Because of this, paleobotanists are able to identify the pollen of centuries-old vegetation with great accuracy.

Timing Is Everything

When a single plant has both male and female flowers, nature must be certain the two do not directly pollinate. To prevent this from happening, a number of systems are used.

Timing is one approach and, in the case of an African water lily, *Nymphae citrina*, the system is as ingenious as it is direct.

The female portion is a deep bowl, containing a thin, sugary liquid, obviously created to attract a variety of insects. The male portion is a flatter area directly above it.

To guarantee cross-fertilization, the two sexes are never open at the same time.

Here's the way it works: At one point, some of the flowers "become" male. The stamens, or male parts, open, forming a hood that covers the female bowl. As insects seek the nectar that they can smell but cannot see, they pass through male pollen that coats their bodies.

At another point, the same flowers "become" female. The male portion is closed, making a platform on which insects can land. Instantly they slide to the middle, where the female bowl is found. Most insects can escape from the liquid-filled bowl and, in escaping, leave behind any pollen on their bodies. In this way, the flower is fertilized and can produce seeds.

Like Attracting Like

Nature has devised many ways to be certain that plants do not self-pollinate. Another example can be found in the thrift, or sea pink (*Armeria maritima*). The secret lies in its pollen and stigma.

While the flowers appear to be exactly the same, closer inspection shows that there are differences—two kinds of pollen (which is the male element) and two types of stigma (part of the female component).

On some plants, the pollen has a coarse surface, while the stigma has a smoother surface.

On other plants, the arrangement is reversed: The pollen is smooth, while the stigma has a rougher surface.

The system works this way: Pollen with a coarse surface matches with a coarse-surfaced stigma, while pollen with a smooth surface matches with a smooth stigma.

Another Protection

In preventing self-pollination, we've seen the power of time and of like attracting like, but nature has also devised another surefire system, as seen in the petunia.

The pollen of many petunias will remain inactive—that is, refuse to germinate—if placed on the stigma of its own flowers.

Yet it will instantly create seed if carried to another plant of the same species.

Saving Pollen

Male pollen, when combined with the female element in the ovary, is the material from which seeds are produced. Pollen is also an ideal food. Since many insects use it to feed their young, plants have had to devise ways of making certain that there is sufficient pollen on hand to produce the next season's flowers.

Many species take a direct approach, producing pollen in such amazing quantities that there is more than enough to go around.

Other plants substitute a less precious commodity. In many cases, this is a sugary nectar that has nothing directly to do with reproduction.

The anthers of *Tripogandra grandiflora*, a common indoor plant in America, substitute "out of date" pollen for the real thing. The pollen taken by insects is old and infertile.

Eria, a species of the epiphyte orchid, uses trickery. It produces a powder that seems like pollen yet is not.

Maxillaria, another epiphyte orchid, also offers an imitation pollen. Most bees seem to prefer it, ignoring the real thing.

Some members of the spiderwort family have become great deceivers. Their anthers are brightly colored to give the impression that they are covered with pollen. Insects attracted there find neither pollen nor any other reward, but by the time they've discovered the trick, they have guaranteed reproduction.

Protection Racket

A number of plants offer neither pollen nor nectar, providing instead an indispensable service.

Calluna vulgaris, the common Scottish heather, has solved the problem of reproduction by protecting male thrips. (Thrips are sucking insects that feed on many plants.)

Male thrips must be numbered among the world's more disadvantaged wimps. They are fewer in number than the females, are less mobile, are unable to fly, and cannot defend themselves. When it is time to mate, the best they can do is hide and the more aggressive females must seek them out. This is where the heather's unusual service enters the picture.

For male thrips, *C. vulgaris* provides an essential protection. Male thrips hide beneath its branches. As the females seek their mates, they collect pollen, and while flying from plant to plant, help to create future generations of flowers.

Mimicry

Still other plants deliberately fool insects. One orchid, *Ophrys speculum*, has petal markings that resemble the female of a species of wasp. Male wasps return again and again to the orchid, thinking they are mating, when in reality they are helping the orchid pollinate and reproduce.

In scientific terminology, such a pollinating process is called *pseudo-copulation*.

Mimicry Explained

Why would an insect want to make love to a flower? Considering the urge versus the opportunity to reproduce, a male often has no choice.

Pseudocopulation is a common method of pollination for the bee orchid, whose flowers open early in the season.

According to nature's timetable, the first bees out and about are male. The females are seen later.

The entire process is a two-way street. The reproductive urge is extremely strong and, short of abstinence, which is not in a bee's vocabulary, the male insects literally have to make do with the orchid. In nature's book, this suits the orchid, since it results in pollination.

Special Plant Markings

The markings on many flowers are not designed to fool a visitor but to help insects find the all-important pollen.

The popular iris has three large, brightly colored *sepals*, or lower petal segments. A very decorative female part called the *crest* is found in the middle.

The crest is divided into three parts, each ending in a frill. The stigma is found there.

If this sounds complicated, imagine how it must seem to a visiting bee. But nature provided help.

To simplify the problem, each crest is decorated with a vibrant pattern of veins. These are routing guides, functioning the same as the colored lines on hospital floors. A bee following the markings is led to the heart of the crest, where it is forced beneath the important center of reproduction.

On the first flower, it departs loaded with pollen.

On the second flower, it leaves behind pollen collected from the first.

The Yucca and the Moth

Yucca is a well-known family of desert plants, which includes everything from the famous Joshua tree of southern California to the Spanish bayonet common in many gardens. It has an unusual look and is the subject of some amazing stories.

None is more surprising than the tale of one desert species, *Pronuba yuccasella*, that enlists the services of a moth.

In the spring, the female moth lays her eggs in the ovary of the yucca's flower.

Once the eggs are laid, the moth scurries around gathering pollen from nearby yucca plants. She deposits the grains around the eggs.

In time, the eggs hatch, producing hungry moth larvae. The tiny insects consume some of the pollen. Although the little larvae are hungry, they are never greedy.

Somehow nature maintains a balance. Every year there is always sufficient pollen to feed the moth larvae with enough remaining to produce new yuccas.

Joshua tree, a tall, branched, aborescent yucca of the southwestern United States. This one was shot in Death Valley, California.

Pollination Bondage

Perhaps this is crass to suggest, but there is evidence to indicate that some elements in nature have more than a passing interest in sadomasochism.

The mosquito plant (*Cynanchum acuminatifolium*) is one example.

The plant, decorated with small, unassuming white flowers, attracts pollinators through the production of nectar.

Many insect species are welcomed, but when one tries to leave, the departing guest is detained by one leg, held in bondage by a strange clip.

The more the insect struggles, the tighter the clip grips. However, if the insect is strong, it may succeed in freeing itself by pulling the clip from its connection.

But freedom has a price. The clip remains firmly attached to the insect's leg.

There are three unusual aspects to the device. First, it has been designed much like a key. Second, when it is pulled free, two bands of pollen come with it. Third, the next time the insect visits a mosquito plant, the process is reversed.

When the insect visits a second mosquito plant, the clip, still attached to its leg, automatically fits into a space on the plant, just as a key slips into a lock.

Once inserted, it is firmly fixed. The only way an insect can become free is by breaking the clip. If this is done, the insect can fly away, leaving behind the clip and its pollen, which, in time, creates seed and a new mosquito plant.

Pollinating Bats

Pollination by bats is common enough in the plant world, especially in South America. There, a species known as templebells (*Smithiantha*) has devised a special way of guaranteeing that bats alone are the pollinating visitors.

The plant's flowers give off a faintly unpleasant odor that turns away most insects but has an instant appeal for bats. As the bats fly around the flowers, pollen is attracted to their fur.

A Surefire Method

Some flowers do not leave pollination to chance, trusting neither to the performance of insects nor birds.

The mountain laurel (*Kalmia latifolia*), for one, has created a reliable and direct approach.

The stamens of the laurel flower are spoked, resembling the frame of an umbrella. The tips are attached to special pouches filled with pollen.

One touch from the smallest insect and the stamens straighten, instantly releasing pollen towards the middle, which is precisely where the visitor can be found.

Trapping Pollinators

Perhaps nature's strangest means of pollination is reserved for the *Ceropegia*, a member of the milkweed family. It attracts insects by scent and sight and features two trapping mechanisms.

The surface of the flower is topped with shimmering hairs, which, because they appear alive, seem to attract insects as much as anything.

The flower also includes a long, erect tube. Two lobes at the top remind one of a lantern. The combination of scent and shimmering light lures flies, which enter the tube just below the lantern.

The tube itself is lined with small hairs that point downwards and are coated with an oily substance. Once they've reached this point, the flies have no foothold. They slide into a chamber at the bottom, where escape is impossible—or so it seems.

In fact, the flies are not doomed. They do not remain trapped, at least not forever. After a few days—or in what must seem like the flower's "own good time" to an impatient insect—the tube begins to droop. Eventually it lies horizontally. The hairs shrivel, the oil dries, and the flies that have survived can escape.

The end result? You guessed it: pollination.

Deceitful Scents

Stapelia, an African cactuslike succulent, lives in an area where flies abound and, because they are the most common airborne commodity, the plant relies on them for propagation.

With nothing concrete to attract flies, offering neither food nor safe haven, it draws them by sleight of hand. Its purple flowers, which grow singly or in clusters, resemble starfish and have the texture and scent of over-aged meat.

To complete the deception, the flowers on most species are flecked with colors also suggesting a rotting appearance. As an added attractant, they are covered with hairs that flicker in the wind.

This flickering gives the impression of thousands of feeding flies, which seems to assure visitors that everything is safe. Carrion flies are lured in large numbers and, finding nothing edible, eventually leave, but not before they have completed pollination.

Catering to Bees

On a happier note, some flowers provide a chance at pure luxury. In one case, the lure is perfume. It is used by male insects to help attract females.

Certain male bees have leg pouches designed to hold drops of scented oil drawn from particular flowers. The oil is the same ingredient as that used in formulating the most costly Parisian perfumes.

Making their rounds, the bees scoop up the perfume, storing it in their pouches. When a pouch is full, the bee flies to a highly visible leaf. Strutting and posturing, he wafts the scent through the air, waiting for female bees to smell it and settle in.

Fruit

The fruits we eat are formed from the ovary of a plant.

A tomato, for example, was once a minute green thing created in the ovary of a tomato pistil. Growing to more than 100,000 times its original size, it changes color and becomes ripe.

Other examples include grapes, peaches, and plums.

Fruit always develops after flowering. In nature's kingdom, there is no other way.

The mushroom we see and eat is the reproductive portion, known to experts as the "fruit body" of the fungal organism, much of which grows underground.

Shameless Plants

Nature never seems embarrassed by sexual implications. Suggestive humor lies only in the mind of man.

For instance, one member of the stinkhorn family is a fungus called *Phallus impudicus*, which appears in late summer throughout England.

Attracting thousands of flies with an odor of decaying flesh, the reproductive process of the fungus is as unusual as other aspects of the plant.

Much of the fungus is covered with an odorous jelly that carries reproductive spores. It is devoured by flies. While the jelly seems tasty, it is also indigestible and is quickly excreted.

The flies merely supply a method of travel. The spores survive the passage, living to generate new plants.

It has been estimated that one speck of jelly excreted by a carrion fly contains enough spores to create 20 million new stinkhorns.

The Importance of Color and Smell

It's a good bet that if insects had no eye for color, there would be no color in flowers. Nature has carefully arranged the many colors and scents of plants to attract special insects, which explains why all plants do not look or smell the same.

Beetles have a better sense of smell than sight, so plants designed to appeal to them have more odor than color. Plants that attract beetles are generally white or light in color.

The color vision of a bee focuses on blues, purples, and yellows. The flowers that attract them are bright and showy.

While birds have a poor sense of smell, they are blessed with superb vision. They can see reds and yellows best and flowers designed to attract them flash those colors.

5
AMAZING SEEDS

What Is a Seed?

A seed is a road map, a construction plan, the beginning of a new plant.

Inside its hard shell, nature has packed everything needed to produce a duplicate of the plant that created the seed.

It develops from a flower. A tomato seed comes from a small white-and-yellow flower that appeared long before any tomatoes.

Bean and pea seeds are found in pods, which are also the product of flowers. Some seeds are found inside shells, some in capsules.

Among the smallest seeds are the almost invisible, dustlike seeds of the orchid. Four million seeds of the *Cynoche* orchid weigh but half an ounce.

The largest is the coconut. The large, tough covering that we break open is its protective shell. The edible meat found inside is the beginning of a new tree.

An Inside Look

If you could separate the inside portion from its hard protective shell, you would discover a small plant waiting to spring to life. As with human babies, the object inside the shell is called an "embryo."

In many seeds, such as beans, peanuts, and peas, two rounded objects fill almost the entire package.

In botanical terms, these are *cotyledons*, a Greek word meaning "cup-shaped hollow."

These odd-looking, cup-shaped bumps will become the first leaves on a new plant.

In some species, such as beans, the tiny cotyledons push through the soil to rise above the surface—the obvious beginnings of the stem, leaves, and so on.

In others, such as peas, they remain below ground. The stem and other portions develop above them.

The process of a seed ripening for growth is called "germination."

Travelling Seeds

When seeds are ready to germinate, they face three serious problems:

- First, they must leave the parent plant.
- Next, they must find some place to make their own way in life, a favorable spot to set up their own housekeeping.
- Finally, they must find a way of getting there.

In order for seeds to disperse, they must somehow travel to new ground. The preferred method is often to utilize one of the intermediate agents tested in pollination: wind, water, or animals.

Of these, the wind is thought to be the first and still the most common.

Many seeds have unique growths that allow them to travel great distances on wind power alone.

One example of these growths is the tiny parachutes found on dandelions (*Taraxacum*) and lettuce (*Lactuca*).

Clematis and anemone makes use of a stylish featherlike plume.

Maple, lime, and ash seeds have "wings."

Slingshot Seeds

Many of the seeds found in pods and capsules have developed their own specialized means of travel.

For some, the pod itself splits when the seeds are ripe, spilling the contents on the ground or, in some cases, shooting them surprising distances.

Poppy seed (*Papaver ssp.*) makes use of an unusual capsule. It has a ring of holes just below the cap. When the wind blows, the capsule shakes and seeds are dispersed through the holes, just like salt from a shaker.

Other seeds have developed more explosive devices.

One common gorse (*Ulex europaeus*) has devised a pod that, when ripe, suddenly twists violently, throwing seeds a considerable distance in all directions.

A balsam called touch-me-not (*Impatiens noli-tangere*) is so sensitive that, when the fruit is ripe, the slightest touch will fling its seeds in a sudden, whirling motion, speedy enough to sting as if flung from a slingshot.

Waterborne Seeds

The shells of many seeds are impervious to water and, like a toy boat, can float miles down a river or stream, all in the hopes of finding a new home.

The coconut shell is so waterproof and buoyant that it can remain afloat for weeks.

Common dandelion (Taraxacum officinale). *When it has developed into seed, it is especially beautiful. Each seed is easily airborne and comes equipped with its own parachute. The slightest breeze can carry one for miles.*

The seeds of some sedges (*Carex*), a large family of grasslike herbs, are protected in water-resistant envelopes.

Seeds That Hitch Rides

Many seeds, using burrs, bristles, hooks, and spines, receive lifts from insects and animals. Some rely on birds. Others find travelling best on the clothing of humans.

Nuts are typical of these seeds voluntarily carried off by animals. Many are hustled away by squirrels and chipmunks. Some are dropped. Others are opened and consumed. Those not immediately needed are often buried.

Squirrels have a poor memory and commonly cannot remember where their winter supplies are hidden, which is exactly what a nut wants. Those buried at the right depth will germinate.

Other seeds have a coating resistant to digestive juices. They can be eaten and eventually excreted, still whole, still in condition to germinate and grow.

Birds transport many seeds. Some are eaten and excreted later. Others stick to their feet.

As an experiment, Charles Darwin grew a magnificent weed garden, more than an acre in size, from seeds taken from the feet of migratory birds.

Fast-Growing

A seed is no indicator of the size of a plant nor the speed at which it grows. Some of the smallest seeds develop into surprisingly large plants.

An Amazon water lily has a normal-sized seed yet ranks among the world's fastest-growing and largest water plants.

It develops from a tiny seed into an adult plant in just seven months.

The leaves are 6 feet long. The flowers are 8 inches in diameter. The stems can be 18 feet long. The plant can even support a small child, as was proved at the Crystal Palace Exhibition in London in 1851.

Petunias are one of the longest-blooming of all garden flowers, often showing color well into autumn. About 30 species are cultivated. The seed is one of nature's smallest, measuring just ¹/₅₀ inch across.

6

HERBS AND POISONOUS PLANTS

The Way We Thought of Plants

Most of our ancestors thought that man was the center of the universe and that everything on our planet was placed here solely for human use. They believed that plants grew strictly for the benefit of people.

Nothing expresses such an anthropocentric attitude better than this quote by an anonymous fifteenth-century German writer: "Many thousands of perils and dangers beset man. He is not fully sure of his health or his life for one moment . . . but the Creator of Nature who has placed us amid such dangers has mercifully provided us with a remedy . . . all kinds of herbs, animals and other created things to which He has given special powers."

Friendly Herbs

It's been said that the English scholar Alcuin (735–804), who taught Charlemagne (742–814) and helped bring a semblance of learning to the Frankish court, once asked the king, "What is an herb?"

The smiling king replied, "A friend of physicians and the praise of cooks."

Charlemagne's pithy answer has stood the test of time.

Herbs have been among the most useful of plants almost since man's beginnings. While we've relied on them for food and medication for centuries, the most common use, then as now, has been in cooking.

Although many varieties were consumed raw while man was still discovering fire, our ancestors quickly discovered that a touch of herbs could add flavor and interest to almost any cooked food. That has been their primary use ever since.

Early Herbal Uses

The first "official" list of herbs that should be planted in a home garden appeared during the reign of Charlemagne.

The Frankish king ordered his subjects to include more than 70 herbs and vegetables in their gardens. Why?

- First, vegetables and herbs were good for one's health.
- Second, most herbs made food tastier.
- Third, some were "lucky"—having the power to ward off dangerous spirits.

Two fourteenth-century cookbooks contain elaborate recipes using nearly all the herbs common today as well as a number no longer grown. *Form of Curry*, an English book focusing on the uses of curry in cooking, and *Le Menager de Paris*, a French book, suggest uses for anise, basil, bay, caraway, dill, marjoram, mint, parsley, sage and many other herbs that would make sense today.

Why Were There So Few Early Cookbooks?

Strange as it seems, researchers can find numerous early manuscripts on the use of plants for medicinal purposes while few describe the preparation of herbs and vegetables for culinary uses. But there is a simple explanation.

The Greeks, who wrote most of the early manuscripts, considered cooking one of the "mechanical" arts, which meant it was unworthy of the attention of those who were educated—and only the educated could write.

Herbal Medicines

While herbs have real use in medications, many of the possibilities suggested over the centuries are based on error, false claims, and pure charlatanry.

At one time, it was thought that plants whose parts resembled something else could have a beneficial effect on something related to whatever they resembled.

For example, it was believed that a plant whose leaves resembled a snake's head could cure venomous bites and that leaves shaped like a heart could cure cardiac disorders.

In those days, many medications extracted from plants were called *nostrums*, a word we've taken to mean a secret cure.

In Latin, the word simply means "ours," in reference to the fact that if there were any benefit, it would be minimal, not worth discussing, and known only to the people who concocted the cure.

Legendary Healing Herbs

Nicholas Culpeper (1616–1654) was well known as an English astrologer and became better known as the father of herbal medicine.

In about 1645 he published *Culpeper's Complete Herbal*, outlining folk remedies based on the use of herbs and plants. A best-seller when it was published, the book is still in print. Many people still swear by the more than 400 pages of somewhat bizarre suggestions. The descriptions that follow, drawn from Culpeper's book, show, if nothing else, how people some 350 years ago believed in the power of nature.

Angelica (*Archangelica ssp.*, "an herb of the sun") should be harvested while the sun is shining, according to Culpeper. It was a comfort for the heart and, when dried and candied, could be used to fight infection. It also cured toothache. (Current gardeners limit its uses to borders.)

Basil (*Ocimum basilicum*, "an herb of Mars") could be used to cure venomous bites. "Laid in dung," Culpeper wrote, "it will breed venomous

LEFT: *Clary sage* (Salvia sclarea) *is a tall flowering plant with coarse foliage. The ancients believed it had power as an eyewash. Culpeper swore that seeds placed in the eyes would clear them from motes as well as remove the red. He also noted that a paste made from the seeds would reduce general swelling and leaves fried in a batter of flour, egg, and milk would cure backache.* RIGHT: *Anise hyssop* (Agastache foeniculum), *also known as giant hyssop. The large, heavily veined leaves are now used mostly in gardens for a bold touch. Hyssop has been considered an "herb of purification." Even today those interested in cult magic use hyssop in baths and sachets for cleansing. Culpeper called it a "violent" purgative. The root was powdered and used in many ways.*

beasts." (Today, basil is used almost exclusively as a seasoning. Common in Italian recipes, it especially enhances dishes with tomato.)

Fennel (*Foeniculum vulgare*) was suggested for a number of ills. Said to promote urine, it was also known to ease the pain of gallstones. When boiled in barley water, it was said to be beneficial to nursing mothers. (Today, its primary use is culinary. Similar to dill in flavoring, it is used in many recipes, from puddings to salads.)

Feverfew (*Chrysanthemum parthenium*) was most often recommended as a "strengthener" during pregnancy. Boiled, the liquid was given to expectant mothers. (Today, it is nothing more than a garden plant.)

Rosemary (*Rosmarinus officinalis*), a well-known Mediterranean herb, was called a plant "of the sun." Oil distilled from the flowering tops was used in perfume and medicine. Culpeper suggested that it could ease rheumy eyes and cure head colds and was an antidote to giddiness.

Early Foods

During the Neolithic age, when gardening first began, many of the plants we know today were cultivated for their edible roots and bulbs. Beets, carrots, radishes, and turnips were among the first.

The most prized by early man was the man-of-earth, a relative of the morning glory and sweet potato. Its roots grow the length of a man and can weigh as much as 15 pounds.

Prehistoric tribes avidly hunted lily bulbs and devoured them both raw and roasted.

The Aztecs and Incas consumed dahlia rhizomes the way people eat potatoes today, as a part of their daily diet.

The Greeks savored the roots of the yellow asphodel (*Asphodeline lutea*). Boiled tulip bulbs are still a popular springtime dish in Crete.

Many American Indians relied on the bulbs of the camas, a species of lily, for food during the summer, while others gathered lewisia, a plant with thick, starchy roots and corms.

Roots of *Lunaria*, best known as honesty, were used in salads in Elizabethan England. The plant was introduced before 1590.

Leaves of the North American plant scarlet bergamot (*Mondara didyma*) were used to make tea, which explains why it is sometimes called the Oswego tea plant.

Manihot glaziovii, a source of Ceara rubber, has been a dietary staple for many South American Indians and it is still cultivated for its starchy roots. We know the product best as tapioca.

Other Uses

The Aztecs and Incas used several bulbs and roots for medicinal purposes.

The roots of *Jatropha*, a small shrub, and *Justica pectoralis*, a shrubby water willow, were used as aphrodisiacs.

The beautiful *Tropaeolum*, the nasturtium or "bitter Indian," was considered an antidote.

The *Stenomesson*, a bulb of the Andes, was issued as a contraceptive.

Datura, or thorn apple, and *Thevetia* were in wide use as anesthetics.

Cabbage

Most experts who have researched the world's earliest plants believe that cabbage was one of man's first domesticated vegetables.

If not, the plant has at least been domesticated for so long that it's hard to know exactly when it began.

Those expert in such matters believe that the original variety was the sea cabbage (*Brassica oleracea*), although no wild species resembling the original variety can be found today.

Although they have different shapes, textures, and colors, broccoli, cauliflower, and kale are merely varieties of the cabbage species.

Lettuce

For generations people have insisted that a little bit of lettuce is good for you. In one manuscript, written during the first century A.D., the Roman writer Pliny the Elder stated that lettuce leaves saved the life of the Roman emperor Augustus, although he didn't explain how.

Lacking refrigeration, the same Romans preserved lettuce, long after the Italian growing season was over, by dousing it in *oxymel*. The term refers to a 2,000-year-old mixture of honey and vinegar.

No one knows how effective it was as a preservative, but, if nothing else, oxymel must rank as the world's first "sweet and sour" dressing.

Today, Americans still argue about the proper point in a meal at which to serve a light lettuce salad. Some believe it should come before the main dish. Others insist the best time is nearer the end of a meal.

If you want to be "Continental," try the end of the meal. In Roman times, lettuce was served just before dessert.

Multipurpose Cumin

Cumin (*Umbelliferae cuminum*) is not only a popular spice, but it has many commercial uses.

It is an essential ingredient in curry powder.

It is used in making kummel, a popular German liqueur, which can also be flavored with anise and caraway.

It is an important seasoning in sauerkraut and some popular German breads.

Dioscorides, an early Greek physician, insisted that cumin made the skin become pale and wan. This information was used by Roman students to fake the "stress and strains" of prolonged study.

Pliny the Elder, always the Roman gossip, said, "It is generally stated that the pupils of Porcius Latro, so celebrated among professors of eloquence, used this drink for the purpose of imitating the paleness their master had contracted through long, difficult study."

Jujube

While most of us associate this word only with a rather gummy, sugary candy, the name is derived from a dried fruit that has a similar consistency.

Originally from China, the plant came to Italy at the time of Augustus (63 B.C.–14 A.D.). In the second century, the Greek medical writer Galen said he could not describe the value of the jujube plant "because the women and children have picked and eaten all of them."

But in the eleventh century, the Arabic philosopher and physician Avicenna told patients that the fruit was good for illnesses of the stomach and lungs.

The English used it to cure gallstones, jaundice, and dropsy.

Juniper

If you are a drinking person, the word "juniper" should bring about an instant and pleasant association—a flavoring in gin.

While the berries are a primary ingredient in better gins, those who insist that juniper is also responsible for the name of the liquor are only partly right.

The term "gin" is derived from "geneva," which in turn was based on a popular misunderstanding of *Juniperus*, the Latin term for the tree on which the berries are grown.

Want to know why people still drink gin? Well, martini lovers aside, in the seventeenth century the English herbalist Nicholas Culpeper swore juniper was a boon to mankind, as it was a cure for venomous bites, cough, consumption, ruptures, cramps, and convulsions. Perhaps that idea still carries over.

Leek

Centuries ago, the common leek (*Allium porrum*) was regarded as more than just a vegetable, especially if you can believe our quotable Roman, Pliny.

According to Pliny, Nero had decided to sing at a public gathering but was unsure of his voice. To improve his vocal cords, Nero consumed at regular intervals prior to his appearance, a preparation of leek and oil, while abstaining from all other food.

Pliny does not comment on the emperor's voice on the night of the concert, so his performance must have gone off well.

On the other side of the coin, a Greek physician insisted that leek gave one nightmares.

Clove

The early Greeks had no name for the spice we call clove, but the Romans called it *clavus* because it resembled a small nail.

Clove, now *Sygzygium aromaticum*, was one of the primary spices in earlier times and a key ingredient in the spice trade, which had been long dominated by the Arab nations.

Clove and other spices were among the reasons Columbus set sail for the west. The explorer hoped to find a new sea route to the rich spice lands of the East, circumventing the costly hold the Arabs had on land routes.

By the sixteenth century, Europeans discovered a sea route around the tip of Africa, and the spice trade, still a major part of commerce, was suddenly dominated by the West, first by the Portuguese and eventually by the Dutch.

Violet

In Greek legend, the most important god, Zeus, created the violet as a special sweet-smelling food for Io, the daughter of the river god Inarches.

Io is the Greek name for the violet. Once Latinized, it became Viola, now the family name for the flower.

The juice from the plant was used to help insomniacs sleep and was thought to cure cardiac patients of weak hearts.

Day Lily

In China the day lily (*Hemerocallis fulva*) was known as the "flower of forgetfulness." An edible plant, a bite or two was thought to cure loss of memory.

Other Lilies

Two species of *Lilium* are among the world's oldest domesticated plants. Prehistoric gatherers used the bulbs as food and ancient Greeks imported

LEFT: *The lily* (Lilium) *comes in a variety of shapes and sizes and has been popular around the world. Most gardeners consider it one of the most stately and elegant of plants. Two species are among the world's oldest domesticated plants. Prehistoric gatherers used the bulbs as food, and ancient Greeks imported them from Asia Minor to make a medicated ointment.* RIGHT: *Blossoms of* Origanum, *better known as marjoram. For those who practise astrology, it is controlled by the planet Mercury and supposedly brings love, happiness, and money. Violets and marjoram, combined and worn close to the skin, are said to protect against colds.*

them from Asia Minor to make a medicated ointment. Later, they were grown throughout Europe as food.

Natural Tranquillizers

An effective tranquillizer is extracted from a member of the dogbane family: *Apocynum*.

A related plant, *Rauwolfia*, is also known for its calming effect on children and adults. Mahatma Gandhi frequently drank a tea made from it.

A Word of Warning

If we humans were to be given dominion over nature, it would seem that one of two other things should also have been true: Either everything around us should have been made safe, or we should have been provided with a natural ability to distinguish the good from the bad. Unfortunately, neither one happened.

Since the appearance of the first of our species, we have been living in close contact with hundreds of plants that can cause irritation, illness, and even death.

A few plants are downright dangerous; a larger number are only moderately so.

Herbs and Poisonous Plants 67

Some can cause skin problems, respiratory problems, or other illnesses that are more the result of allergenic reactions than toxicity.

A number of these plants are found in our gardens, attractive flowers and shrubs prized for their usefulness in landscaping.

Even certain fruits and vegetables that we eat have some degree of toxicity.

Common foods, such as apples, asparagus, castor beans, and peaches, contain parts that are highly poisonous if consumed in excess.

The seeds in apples and those inside a peach stone contain cyanide.

Asparagus spears contain mercaptan, a substance that, if taken in large amounts, can cause irritation.

Castor beans contain a highly toxic component.

Neither animals nor birds will touch mistletoe leaves or stems because they are poisonous. However, birds can consume the berries without harm.

The Most Dangerous Poison

What is the most dangerous natural poison? In North America, it may be the poisonous hemlock plant (*Conium maculatum*). Although its poison is especially virulent, the plant appears to be harmless, as it closely resembles wild carrot, parsley, and parsnip.

A second choice might be the South American lana tree. Indians use its sap to make curare, a most dangerous tarry substance with which they tip their arrows. It brings death in a matter of minutes.

First Hallucinogenic

We've heard of hallucinogenic mushrooms and other hallucinogens, but what is the first instance of man's use of a plant for this purpose?

It probably occurred at a time so remote in history that no one knows, but one of the first recorded notations comes from the first-century Greek physician Dioscorides.

Writing of *Datura ssp.*, the thorn apple, the Greek said, "The root being drunk in the quantity of a dram has the power to effect not unpleasant fantasie. Two being drunk makes one beside himself for three days. Four being drunk will kill him."

The thorn apple is one of more than a dozen varieties in a family that includes tobacco, belladonna, and mandrake. It originated in Asia and can be found in the United States.

One variety in the United States is *Datura stramonium*, the infamous jimson weed known to kill cattle.

A tropical species found in California and Florida is *D. meteloides*, known as "the angel's trumpet." It is one of a number of hallucinogenic alkaloids and its narcotic, medicinal, and poisonous properties are well certified.

In moderation, it dilates pupils. In overdose, it produces dizziness and deliriums.

Early Californian Indian tribes used it in their puberty rites to produce a stupor.

Some Poisonous Plants

What follows are some of the less obvious plants known to cause problems. You might want to keep the list handy.

Amaryllis belladonna, belladonna lily   The bulb is dangerous.

Arisaema triphyllum, jack-in-the-pulpit   The plant contains needlelike crystals of calcium oxalate that can cause intense irritation. While all parts are dangerous, the roots are the worst.

Buxus sempervirens, common box   The leaves are poisonous.

Convallaria majalis, lily of the valley   The leaves and flowers are poisonous.

Daphne ssp., daphne   The bark, fruit, and leaves are extremely dangerous. A few berries can kill a child.

Dieffenbachia seguine, dumb cane   The leaves and stems can cause intense irritation.

Digitalis purpurea, foxglove   The leaves can cause digestive distress and mental confusion.

Helleborus niger, Christmas rose   The leaves and roots can cause skin problems.

Hyacinthus, hyacinth   The bulb, which can cause vomiting and nausea, may even be fatal.

Impatiens ssp., impatiens   The young leaves and stems are moderately dangerous.

Lobelia ssp., lobelia   The leaves, fruit, and stems may cause skin irritation.

Papaver somniferum, opium poppy   The unripe seed pod is extremely dangerous.

Rhododendron ssp., rhododendron and azalea   The leaves and other parts can be fatal.

Solanum tuberosum, Irish potato   Believe it or not, the green part just below the skin can be dangerous.

Thevetia pueruviana, yellow oleander   All parts are dangerous.

Wisteria, wisteria   Several parts of the plant are dangerous, especially for children. The most common symptom is severe indigestion.

LEFT: *Belladonna* (Atropha belladonna), *known also as deadly nightshade, is common to Asia and the Mediterranean and is an extremely poisonous plant. The main ingredient is atropine, an alkaloid found in much of the genus* Solanaceae. *Belladonna means "beautiful lady" in Italian. The name is derived from the fact that belladonna was used in early cosmetics.* RIGHT: *The famed opium poppy* (Papaver somniferum). *Opium is made from the pods.*

Emergency First Aid

If problems occur with any of the plants in the preceding list, these are the recommended procedures:

- Call a physician immediately.
- Give a tablespoon of salt dissolved in water to induce vomiting—but only when a patient is conscious. *Never attempt to give liquids to an unconscious person.*
- Keep the patient warm.
- If the patient is not breathing, try artificial respiration.
- If you cannot reach a physician, call an emergency-service number or take the patient to the closest hospital.

7

FASCINATING FLOWERS

Love of Flowers

While man's first interest in the products of nature was focused on plants he could use as religious symbols as much as food, an awareness of flowers for their beauty still goes back thousands of years.

Since the earliest nomads formed societies and then civilizations, flowers have played a significant role in our lives.

In ancient Egypt and China, flowers were held in high esteem, and they were grown as rooftop decorations in the Aztec and Inca civilizations.

Flowers have come to represent everything from the moment of the Creation, as they do in Chinese Taoism, to the Crucifixion of Christ.

The Lily—"Second-Best" Flower?

In the thirteenth century the lily was considered the "second-best" flower in any garden. An English writer of the period, one Bartholomew, wrote, "The lily ranks next to the rose in worthiness and nobleness."

The author was only echoing earlier writers. From the early Greeks to Pliny the Elder, the sentiments were similar.

Although the fragrant, stately rose has been everyone's favorite, the lily has legendary status.

According to one legend, it sprang from the barren ground as Eve shed a tear upon leaving the Garden of Eden. Where the tear fell, a lily suddenly emerged.

Halfway around the world, a Korean legend says much the same thing. When an Androcles-like hero removed a thorn from a tiger, the two became friends. Years later, as the tiger lay dying, the feline begged his human friend to use his magic to keep him nearby. The man did—creating the tiger lily.

In parts of England people once believed that the smell of a lily produced freckles.

Flowers—Not Always As They Appear

We tend to think of the pretty blooms in our gardens as individual flowers. Size is unimportant. When we see one, whether large or small, most of us consider that it is just that—a single flower.

Not always. Sometimes a bloom that seems to be an individual flower is actually a number of smaller ones grouped to give the appearance of a larger bloom.

Nature does this to be certain that the plant attracts sufficient pollinating insects. One large flower attracts potential pollinators more readily than smaller ones.

Examples can be found in the composite (*Compositae*) family. The large and showy "flower" one sees at dahlia exhibits, for instance, is actually a group of numerous smaller versions.

In some species, there are two kinds of flower. The sunflower is typical. Its face has a disc surrounded by rays. The disc is actually one type of flower and the rays are another.

Anthemis cotula, *a member of the genus* Compositae, *includes some hundred subspecies of herbs. Known as dog fennel or mayweed, it can be found growing wild in many areas and is popular with gardeners who specialize in "wild" gardens.*

The Importance of Darkness and Light

Botanists often describe plants in terms of their demand for light. The hours of light a plant receives has an effect on the way it flowers. It is this factor botanists measure.

There are *short-day*, *intermediate*, and *long-day* plants.

A short-day plant requires less than 12 hours of light to produce flowers. Chrysanthemum, poinsettia, and Christmas cactus are examples.

Long-day plants, such as many of those native to the North Temperate Zone, may not bloom unless they receive 12 to 16 hours of light. The Chinese aster is typical.

Intermediate plants, those insensitive to periods of illumination, fall someplace in between.

Darkness Is Important, Too

New research indicates that the hours of darkness may be as important to a plant as periods of sunlight.

Sunlight does have an effect, but new studies have shown that the length of darkness, short or long, also helps to influence the way a plant blooms.

Scientists are not certain of the procedure but suspect that the lighted period creates a hormone in the leaves that is transported to the growth areas, creating buds and flowers.

The dark period is important because it "sets the plant," meaning that it gives it a rest and reinforces and establishes the pattern.

Why Plants Are Green

Most of us know that it's the chlorophyll that makes plants green, but that's only part of the explanation.

The rest of the answer lies in light itself.

Sunlight is "white," a mixture of a rainbow of colors. Plants absorb most of the light. The color they do not absorb is green. It is reflected; we see the reflection and that explains why plants appear green.

The same concept explains why colored blossoms appear in their respective colors. For instance, a red rose absorbs all other colors, reflecting red.

What's a Weed?

To the true scientist, there is no such thing.

To a naturalist, almost everything is beautiful. One man's weed is another man's flower. A field of dandelions, buttercups, speedwells, and daisies can be every bit as lovely as the rarest orchid.

But if you define a "weed" as anything that has become a nuisance, then even the most beautiful of flowers can be called a weed. And that unfortunate circumstance occurs more often than you might suspect.

For instance, in Australia a popular Mediterranean plant, the "viper's bugloss" (*Echium plantagineum*), was introduced as a garden flower at just one ranch. But within eight years, it had gotten out of hand, spreading a distance of more than 500 miles.

Old Favorites

Many flowers have been popular in gardens and used for medication and flavorings for centuries.

Jerusalem cross (*Lychnis chalcedonica*) has long been a popular garden companion. It was seen in ancient Turkish gardens some time before the Christian era and was probably introduced to Europe at the time of the Crusades.

Double-flowered forms were created and introduced in England by 1629.

Artemisia has been a garden favorite since early Roman times and has been used in many ways:

- as a moth killer
- in medicine
- as a love potion
- to flavor numerous foods and beverages

Peripatetic Tulips

If you like tulips, pause for a moment to thank two sixteenth-century pioneers, Ogier Chislaine de Busbecq and Charles de l'Ecluse. (The latter is also known to flower lovers as Carolus Clusis of Artois.)

De Busbecq was a keen amateur botanist and ambassador from the Holy Roman Empire to Suleiman the Magnificent, the Ottoman sultan. Long before the ambassador arrived, tulips had been a favorite throughout the Ottoman Empire.

When the ambassador saw them, he sent a parcel of bulbs to Vienna, where they were successfully grown.

A writer and botanist, Clusis sent the first bulbs ever seen elsewhere to England. Within four years, they were the rage there, also.

Their name is derived from the Turkish word *dulband*, meaning turban, which a full-petalled tulip resembles.

During the fifteenth century, they were known as "tulipas." The word has since been shortened.

The World's Most Expensive Flowers

The honor probably goes to the tulip, the hyacinth, and some orchids.

In the sixteenth century, there was a very real "tulip mania" throughout Europe and bulbs sold for hundreds of dollars. In some cases, estates changed hands for a single plant.

In Holland, one rare bulb was traded for 36 bags of corn, 72 bags of rice, 4 fat cows, 12 sheep, 8 pigs, 2 barrels of wine, 4 barrels of beer, 2 tuns of butter, 2 pounds of cheese, and a silver cup—in its time, the list added up to a fortune.

In one of the most famous transactions, a scarlet-and-white-striped *Semper Augustus* tulip was sold for 5,500 florins, more than $70,000 in today's currency.

In 1774, hyacinths were the rage, and one bulb of a variety known as "King of Great Britain" was sold for £100. In the United States, considering inflation and today's values, that would add up to more than $200,000.

Today, most bulbs can be purchased for less than one dollar.

A Most Expensive Dinner

A story is told of a Dutch bulb farmer whose cook, thinking he was using onions, accidentally made a stew of some very costly tulip bulbs. The mistake was not discovered until the farmer finished the last spoonful of what he said was "an excellent meal."

When the loss was totalled, the man judged that the meal had cost him 100,000 gold florins, a fortune valued in today's terms at nearly half a million dollars.

Tulips: Still a Delicacy

Tulips are natives of Turkey, Afghanistan, and Persia and were naturalized over much of Greece in early times. On Crete, where four species still grow, boiled bulbs are a delicacy. They're available in local markets every spring.

Geranium. Shown here is an extremely popular cultivated variety, Martha Washington (Pelargonium domesticum). *The family is known as* Geraniaceae *and includes more than 300 plant species, both annuals and perennials.*

The Orchid and How It Got Its Name

The underground root system of one genus of orchid common in parts of Europe from the earliest times consists of paired, roundish tubers. Nearly 2,000 years ago, the Greek medical writer Dioscorides stated in an offhand manner that the bulbs reminded him of the male genital gland. Accordingly he named the plant *orchis*, which is the Greek word for "testicle."

In later centuries, the name was transferred from the single genus and broadened to include the entire family. You can find it in use now both in the botanical name, *Orchidaceae*, and in the common name, orchid.

One of the Largest Families

Numbering more than 25,000 species, orchids comprise one of the world's largest families of flowering plants. The number does not include thousands of man-made hybrids created by amateurs and professionals.

Although most of us associate the plants with the tropics, varieties can be found in virtually every part of the globe, with the exception of two areas: the desert and polar regions.

Everybody's Orchid

While many orchids seem rare and exotic, there is one species almost everyone knows: the *Cattleya*.

This is the variety florists commonly feature. You can see it at graduation ceremonies, weddings, and elsewhere.

Not Your Standard Orchid

While most of us think of orchids as showy and delicate, some species are anything but. The bamboo orchid, native to Malaysia and the Himalayas, can reach heights of 8 feet. At the top is a small, not very orchidlike flower. The plant has a reedlike appearance and could pass for a member of the bamboo family.

Guaranteeing Pollination

Most orchids go to extremes to bring about cross-fertilization. Because of the way some parts of the plant are arranged, the pollen packet carried by a visiting insect must be in just the right spot before it can adhere to the stigma on the next plant the insect visits. Interior components of the orchid itself are arranged so that one part of the plant is forced forward and down, striking an insect at exactly the proper angle and implanting the pollen in precisely the proper position.

For botanists, the most interesting habit of many species is the manner in which the ovary moves just before the plant opens. Prior to opening, the stemlike ovary executes a half-circle turn, reversing the position of specific flower parts and revealing a conspicuous lip—an inviting "landing strip" for pollinators.

Orchid Seeds: Solving a Problem

Compared with many seeds, orchid seeds are distinctly disadvantaged, but nature has solved this problem rather neatly with a delicately balanced cooperative arrangement in what might otherwise be a situation deadly enough to end the species.

The problem begins with the orchid seed. Possibly because of its small size, it does not contain sufficient nutrition to carry an embryo through to germination. But a cooperative, or symbiotic, venture with a deadly fungus has taken care of the problem.

The symbiosis, which is another way of saying "mutual aid," does not begin with much promise. The fungus—and the species varies with the orchid—first seeks out the seed with the obvious intention of attacking it and making off with the essential oils and nutrition the seed contains.

In a mysterious manner, not yet fully understood, the orchid seed quickly counterattacks, digesting some of the fungus. Within a short time, the attacked becomes the attacker and, for a period, the orchid becomes a parasite, surviving off the fungus.

But the "meal" would not last long enough for a seed to fully germinate, and somehow the orchid seed senses this. What is needed is a delicate balance. If the fungus were too aggressive, it would overpower the seed; if the seed were too strong, it would lose its meal ticket.

Somehow nature creates a precarious balance. The fungus survives off the seed's outer tissue, while on the inside the seedling, utilizing a part of the fungus, matures. The two survive to meet again.

To further complicate matters, this symbiosis does not work with every type of fungus. A special type is needed for each orchid, and somehow nature sorts this all out.

Slow-Growing

Orchids are not noted for fast growth or quick blooming. The development from seed to flowering plant is generally a slow and tedious process.

Certain orchids do not reach their blooming stage for six to nine years.

The record is probably held by a famous species, the lady slipper (*Cypripedium ssp.*). The first flowers appear only after a wait of 15 to 17 years!

A Long Life

While many orchids require years to flower, they compensate on the other end with a long life.

Some orchids have a life expectancy similar to that of humans.

Longevity applies to their flowers as well. Orchid blossoms last longer than almost any other flower—unless they have been fertilized.

Once the blossoms are fertilized, certain chemicals activated by the pollen create a condition causing a quick wilt.

The Narcissus: an Early Garden Flower

Popular with early Egyptians and Greeks, the narcissus ranks as one of the world's first garden flowers.

For example, one variety, *Narcissus poeticus*, has a history stretching back to ancient Greece. It was mentioned in 320 B.C. by Theophrastus, a Greek philosopher, scientist, and disciple of Aristotle.

Another variety, the pleasantly perfumed "paper white" (*N. papyraceus*), was popular in England by the mid 1550s. It was so much in demand that Dutch nurserymen created more than 300 cultivars. A springtime favorite, paper white was common in Victorian drawing rooms.

Most Highly Developed Flowers

Which flowers are considered the most developed? Which rank highest on the evolutionary scale? Believe it or not, the humble and despised dandelion is one. It shares honors as being the culminating product of floral evolution with a couple of other well-known plants—the orchid and crabgrass.

Floral Successes

Generally speaking, plants with the more modest flowers are the most successful in terms of expanding their territory, in covering the planet with their species.

Those with showier flowers commonly have a more limited range.

A Useful Flower

Several species of amaranth are extremely popular with gardeners because the flowers have so many uses.

They can be grown in a garden, displayed as cut flowers, and preserved and dried.

In parts of Asia, some species are grown as vegetables. The seeds are edible and tasty.

Rare Forget-Me-Not

What is the rarest forget-me-not? One good bet is a plant also known as the Chatham Island lily (*Myosotidium hortensis*).

It is found wild only on that one small Pacific island some 500 miles east of New Zealand.

The plant is unusual because it has large funnel-shaped leaves that capture rain, directing it or other available moisture straight to the plant's roots, wasting not one drop.

Boxwood

While boxwood, of the family *Buxus*, a group of 30 evergreen shrubs, may not be exclusively English, it has been common in England, as throughout much of Europe, since Neolithic days.

Charcoal from burned boxwood dating back to Neolithic times has been identified in Great Britain.

It has been found at Roman sites throughout Britain and sprays of the plant were discovered in three early coffins. Since this practice was not common in Rome, archeologists believe that it must have been a local custom.

In later England, sprigs of boxwood were used at funerals. They were placed beside the door so that people could take a spray and, at the proper time, throw it into the grave.

Roman Topiary

On the subject of boxwood, pre-Christian Romans were extremely fond of topiary—evergreen shrubs cut and shaped into artificial forms.

When the Romans invaded England during the time of the Caesars, box was extremely popular. It was used for topiary and many fanciful designs were reported.

World's Largest Flower Show?

Without a doubt, it is the Chelsea Flower Show, sponsored by the Royal Horticultural Society and held in London annually.

The show has taken place for more than 70 years and is held on the grounds of the Royal Hospital in London's Chelsea section.

Its official name: The Great Spring Flower Show. Flowers are exhibited in tents and, even on Member's Day, more than 40,000 visitors pass through.

Exhibitors and visitors come from around the world.

8
MORE FLOWERS

Camellia

The camellia, a member of the tea family (*Theaceae*) was named for a Jesuit priest and botanist, Georg Kamel. The "K" was changed to a "C," when the name was Latinized (into Camellus), since there is no "k" in the Latin alphabet.

As a missionary, Fr. Kamel discovered the plant in China and sent seeds to friends in France.

They were introduced into England in about 1740, the same year they were brought to America by André Michaux.

Camellias were the favorite plants of Chinese mandarins.

Carnation

In Elizabethan England, carnations were loved, hated, and known by several names.

In Shakespeare's *Henry IV*, Falstaff could not "bear the carnation." The color offended him.

In *The Winter's Tale*, Perdita admired them. "The fairest flower of the season," she called them.

In that time, they were best known as gilovre and gillyflower.

In Chaucer's time (1340–1400), they were called "sops in wine," not for what one did with them but for their color.

By 1630 as many as 50 varieties were popular in England.

What might have been the most popular variety? A plant with the strange name of "great grey hullo."

Clematis

The flower's name is derived from the Greek word *klema*, which means a vine branch and can refer to almost any type of climbing plant.

A native of China, clematis was introduced to England by the botanist-explorer Robert Fortune. Since 1835, it has been at home throughout Great Britain, where the light-blossomed *Clematis montana* has long been a wondrous sight running wild through old orchards.

Delphinium

It is difficult to believe that the stately delphinium is related to the lowly buttercup, but it is. Both are members of the family *Ranunculacae*.

The name is attributed to the Greek doctor Dioscorides, who thought that the flower's closed buds resembled a dolphin.

The British name is larkspur, derived from its horn-shaped nectary.

In Dutch, it is *ridden spooren*, or "knight's spur."

Dutchman's Pipe

Aristolochia durior (a.k.a. *A. macrophylla*) was unknown in Europe until it was discovered along the Ohio River by the British plant-explorer John Bartram.

It is an unusual species in many ways. The plant is a climbing vine and its U-shaped blossoms are sometimes two feet wide and nearly a foot long.

Parts of the plant are scented and its roots remind one of camphor.

The flowers are as remarkable as they are unusual because they resemble a meerschaum pipe—hence, the plant's common name.

Gardeners love Dutchman's pipe because it grows fast and climbs well. In a short time, it can be tall enough and wide enough to screen a porch.

There are more than 200 species. Tropical varieties are generally grown in a greenhouse. Hardier types can safely remain outside year-round.

Cultivated dahlias are popular with gardeners.

Hellebore

Centuries ago an English writer described the plant as having a sinister look and a faintly unpleasant scent.

The name itself comes from two Greek words, *helein*, "to kill," and *bora*, "food."

Hellebore has a long domestic history and was mentioned by Hippocrates, perhaps the most celebrated physician of ancient Greece. He practised medicine on the island of Cos 400 years before Christ.

According to legend, the plant was used by Proetus, king of Argos, to cure his daughters of the disturbing delusion that they had been changed into cattle.

Hibiscus

The family of flowers we know as "hibiscus" must be one of the most all-inclusive in the plant world. There are some 250 species and its members represent almost every form of plant we know—herbs, garden flowers, small shrubs, and even trees.

A few species are used for food, fibre, and even medical products.

Cannabinus l., better known as Indian hemp or "bastard jute," produces a fibre that is used commercially. In Africa, oil from the plant is used for burning.

Macrophyllus, Roxb. ex Hornem, is a stately tree, reaching heights of 80 feet.

Still other varieties include the beautiful garden plants known as rose mallow and giant mallow.

Iris

Since Iris was the Greek goddess of the rainbow and the Greeks believed that the flower had borrowed its stunning colors from the sky, the name seems appropriate.

The history of the plant dates at least to 1950 B.C., when Thutmosis I, pharaoh of Egypt, brought bulbs back from Syria as part of his spoils of war. At that time, they were valued as highly as precious metals.

The king thought so highly of his treasure that he had the event depicted on a carved marble panel. It can be seen to this day on the walls of the temple of Ammon at Karnak.

The species represented in those panels is probably *Iris oncocyclus* or *L. Orientalis*.

A powder made from iris root (*I. florentina*, the fleur-de-lis) was common in the Middle Ages. Smelling faintly like violets, it was used as medicine and a household scent.

In Japan, the iris gardens at Horikiri were world-famous.

Madonna Lily

In the lore of the Christian Church, *Lilium candidum*, noted for its strong scent and aristocratic air, is a classic, an emblem of purity associated with the Virgin Mary.

In Roman times, the flower was widely planted and its bulb was used for healing wounds.

Magnolia

Although the magnolia is one of the oldest flowering trees, it did not receive its scientific name until the 1700s, when it was named in honor of Pierre Magnol, a well-known horticulturist who was the respected director of a botanical garden in Montpellier, France.

Prior to receiving its name, the tree was known as the laurel-tulip tree. A native of Asia, it was first grown in England in 1789.

Passionflower

A native of Colombia with more than 400 species, the plant was brought to Europe by the conquistadors (early Spanish explorers).

The plant was so named because of the unique appearance of its flowers, which were seen as symbolizing the Passion, or final sufferings, of Christ.

The stigma represents the nails driven through His hands and feet. The stamens represent His wounds. The red inner corona is His Crown of Thorns. And the 10 lobes of the flower represent those of His apostles who neither denied nor betrayed Him.

Peony

Long touted for its medical values, the peony has been known by numerous names. The Germans called it *pfingsrose*, or Whitsun rose.

The prettiest of the older names is probably the one used in China—*sho-yo*. It simply means "the beautiful."

Since early times, the roots and seeds have been prescribed for pregnant women.

In England it was recommended for "diverse women's sicknesses."

Doctors even recommended it for epilepsy. Said one, "Hang a root about the neck and it will save him, without a doubt, in 15 days."

9
TREES AND GRASSES

What's a Tree?

One encyclopedia defines it as a woody perennial of at least 20 feet in height.

That is not much of a requirement. A number of tropical ferns and some cacti grow substantially taller.

Useful Trees

"Trees and forests are supposed to be the supreme gift nature bestowed on man," wrote Pliny. "We use them to sail the seas and for building houses. Even the images of the gods are carved in them."

The Importance of Bark

While a tree trunk is basically an oversized flower stem (or a flower stem a smaller tree trunk), it is tough, rugged, complex, and essential. The central portion, which we think of as "wood," is actually a network of tubing called *xylem* (from a Greek word meaning "wood"). It varies greatly with the species, but all types carry minerals up and down and disperse useful "foods" made by the process of photosynthesis.

The manner in which bark is created is most interesting. In a variety like the cork oak, it is formed through changes in the outer cells of the branches and the trunk. The cells divide and divide again, until they've created a hard, protective layer.

As with human skin, the exterior layer is called the *epidermis*.

As the exterior hardens, the cells of which it is composed begin to change. The walls become impregnated with a fatty material that botanists call *suberin*. It makes the walls impervious to water.

The Legendary Plane: an Early Favorite

The plane tree, similar in appearance to our sycamore, was a favorite in ancient times, mostly because, given enough water, it grew to tremendous heights.

Greeks and Romans honored it. Both Homer and Virgil mentioned it with admiration.

Agamemnon, a powerful Greek king and one of the Homeric heroes, supposedly planted one at Delphi.

The satyr Marsyas was tied to one, when Apollo flayed him alive for challenging the god to a musical contest and losing.

And Xerxes, on his expedition against Greece, tarried an entire day in Lydia because he could not resist the magnificent shade of a gigantic plane.

A forest near Seaside, Oregon.

In the Beginning

In the earliest times on our planet, the situation was reversed. Trees were much shorter, often the size of common plants, while many ferns were taller than the trees.

By the Devonian period, tree ferns were prolific shallow-water plants, reaching heights of 100 feet.

Mountain Ash

One of a group of 85 species, the mountain ash (*Sorbus ssp.*) has long been thought to have special powers.

The Druids of England planted the tree near their ancient stone circles to ward off evil spirits.

In Scandinavian mythology, Yggdrasil, "the World Tree," was thought to be a species of ash. Even today, numerous superstitions are connected with it.

In England an ash with a trunk that was cleft—that is, which had a natural opening—was believed to be especially powerful. Children were passed through the cavity to cure them of rupture or rickets.

The ancient Greeks prescribed dried berries from the tree as a cure for diarrhea.

A "True" Tree?

The English word "tree" has a close link with an earlier word, the base word of "true." It developed from two earlier English words, "troewe" and "trywe." Both referred to "true" as meaning "firmly planted like a tree."

Sacred Trees

In ancient China, a sacred tree stood in every village. Because residents believed the soul of the town's founder lived in it, the tree was protected and revered.

In the Philippines, early islanders believed that their ancestors inhabited special "soul-carrier" trees. These could not be cut.

Centuries ago, many Europeans believed that a pear tree could protect their cattle and homes. One was conspicuously planted beside every house. As fall approached, if the tree was small, it was brought into the house. If it was large, a few branches were brought in. Just as Christmas trees are decorated today, these trees were given a position of honor and decorated with candies and cheese.

Trees of Gods

Ancient Greeks and Romans believed that certain trees were reserved for specific gods:

- The bay was the tree of Apollo.
- The oak was special to Jupiter.
- The poplar was the tree of Hercules.
- Vines, especially grapevines, were associated with Bacchus.
- A pine sapling was the symbol of Attis, a Phrygian god and consort of Cybele, "mother of gods."

Identifying Cedar

Many people make the mistake of classifying almost any conifer (that is, an evergreen that produces cones) as a cedar, when chances are good that some of them may be junipers.

One sure way of differentiating the two is to remember that the fruit of a juniper is like a berry while the fruit of a cedar is a cone.

However, the two have similarities and there may even be some confusion in the Old Testament.

In the Old Testament, the cedar was seen as a symbol of power, prosperity, and longevity.

The most famous cedar is the biblical "cedar of Lebanon" (*Cedrus libani*). In the Old Testament, it's considered "excellent above all trees of the field."

It is said that Solomon employed 80,000 wood cutters to harvest cedars from local forests. With such an enormous work force, it is a wonder that any have survived—but they have.

The most famous grove of cedars can be found just outside war-torn Beirut, about 15 miles from town.

The first European to see the famous cedars might have been a Frenchman, Pierre Belon, a scientist who visited the Middle East in 1550 to conduct research for the world's first book about cone-bearing trees, *De Arboris Coniferis*.

Eucalyptus

Australia, at the time of its settlement, was a primitive country, noted for strange animals and unusual trees. One of its tallest trees was the giant eucalyptus.

The first European to see the species was the English explorer-botanist Joseph Banks, who was associated with Kew Gardens.

Cork Oak

For centuries the bark of the cork oak was harvested to make stoppers for bottles and insulation in thermos jugs. Since plastics have taken over, the market for real cork has been reduced. Perhaps wine bottles and certain industrial uses reflect the last reliable sales. Today, the tree is grown commercially only in Spain.

The tree is unusual because it is the only one that can survive when the bark is removed. This is because the cork oak is the only tree with a double bark, an outer protective coating and an inner layer that contains the delicate growth cells.

The outer layer is harvested about once every eight years.

A Most Amazing Oak

Not many people have heard of the shrubby kermes oak (*Quercus coccifera*), although for centuries it played an important role in history and medication.

The name is derived from the Arabian word for "crimson."

The "berries" produced by the tree have long been used to make a dye.

This dye was possibly the first coloring to be used by man and was even mentioned by Moses.

The dye was replaced after the discovery of the New World, when the Spaniards returned with cochineal, an insect that could produce a similar and less expensive dye.

But experts have since discovered that the kermes "berry" is not a fruit but a gall caused by an insect closely related to the cochineal.

At one stage, the insects swarm over the kermes plant. In the next, they become inactive, producing eggs and a red juice. At this point, they are collected and dried and then turned into an important medicine.

The ancient Romans made a paste that, when diluted with vinegar, was used to heal wounds.

During the Middle Ages, the dye was also diluted to make a medication called *confection alkermes*. Known to be a useful astringent, its name and the process were officially listed for centuries in the *London Pharmacopeia*.

Pomegranate

The fruit of this tree may be little more than a novelty in the United States, but in the tropics it is both an important part of man's diet and a prized symbol. Worldwide, it ranks as one of the oldest cultivated foods.

It was harvested in prehistoric times and is mentioned in the Song of Solomon: "I would cause thee to drink the spiced wine of the Pomegranate."

It was often used in ancient Hebrew ceremonies and the pattern of the fruit was embroidered on the robes of the high priests as a sign of rank and esteem.

The multipointed calyx that can be seen at the base of the fruit was said to have provided the model for Solomon's crown.

In China, its many seeds are believed suggestive of fertility and the fruit has been the subject of many poems.

A century ago newly married Turkish women would throw the fruit against the ground. They believed that the number of children they would bear could be divined from the number of seeds that fell to the earth.

The Almond

A relative of both the peach and prune, the tree is a native of the Middle East and possibly the Mediterranean, where it thrives.

For the Romans, it was a luxury food. Cato called the fruits "Greek nuts," more for identification than derision, and Pliny swore that almond paste could cure 29 disorders.

A concoction called "almond milk," made with raisins, sorrel, violet and strawberry leaves, buglose, and rosemary, was supposed to be "good for what ails you."

A mixture made from bitter almonds supposedly alleviated intoxication.

Fastest-Growing Tree

If anyone ever asks you the name of the fastest-growing tree, say the acacia and you'll be right.

Several varieties grow as much as 10 feet in four months. That's a rate of 2½ feet a month, or slightly more than an inch a day.

Many species can reach heights of 25 feet in as little as six years.

Most are mature at 30 years. In "tree time" that is short-lived, when you consider that many species reach ages of 100 years or more.

Why wouldn't you say bamboo? Because it is not a tree. It's a grass.

Showiest Tree

What is the showiest tree? Many people would pick the catalpa, also known as the catawba and the "Indian bean." The family includes 13 species, some capable of reaching heights of 50 feet, given sufficient time.

Their appeal comes from the beautiful 8-inch blooms that decorate the tips of their branches.

Those who disagree might substitute the flowering dogwood (*Cornus florida*). In the spring, it is covered with beautiful 3-inch blooms, ranging from white to a magenta-pink. In the fall, it is covered with coral-red fruit.

The Grasses

While grasses may seem beneath concern, lowly, monotonous, and ever so common, they are far more intriguing and varied than you probably imagine. In fact, the grouping is so large that it includes more than a single family.

Although true grasses are found in the botanical family *Gramineae*, botanists categorize grasses in the following ways:

- Horticultural grasses—"ornamentals," which include grasses used in lawns and in decorative ways throughout a garden and in landscaping.
- Forage grasses—longer varieties, grown in pastures to feed animals.
- Timber grasses—commercial treelike grasses, such as bamboo.
- Food grasses—edible grains, from wheat to corn.
- Aromatic grasses—those that produce oils used in making perfumes.

A common prairie grass.

Edible Grasses

The Lord's Prayer speaks of our daily bread and much of our regular food comes from the seeds of grasses—wheat, rye, oats, barley, corn (which, though it doesn't appear so, is a grass), and others.

What makes grass seeds so special? Many are surprisingly rich in carbohydrates, fats, and proteins. Other seeds (we know some as nuts) are rich in fats and oils. Examples include peanuts, walnuts, and even flax and cotton.

Tallest Grass

While we think of grasses as primarily low-growing, at least one species can grow taller than many trees.

The giant bamboo (*Dendrocalamus nees*), a member of the true grass family, reaches heights of 50 feet.

Originally from Asia, most bamboos are extremely drought-resistant and are ideal for the drier parts of the United States.

From the earliest times, bamboo has been important to the life and economy of the Orient.

One Japanese sage wrote, "There is not a necessity, a luxury or a pleasure which bamboo cannot satisfy."

The Busy Rushes

Some 300 species of rush are among our best examples of bog-loving grasses. We have little to do with them now, but in ancient times rushes were used for everything from the thatching of roofs to easy-to-clean bedding.

In Greece they were carved to produce musical pipes.

As helpful as they are, they are sometimes confused with other plants. In the Old Testament, it says that the baby Moses was found in a clump of "bulrushes"—probably not the same thing; the bulrushes of biblical times were most likely a species of papyrus.

Jesus' Crown of Thorns

It is thought that the crown of thorns that the Roman soldiers placed on Jesus' head before His crucifixion was in part made of a species of rush called *Juncus balticus*.

It's believed that the rushes were used to make a circlet that fit over the head and that sticky, blood-shedding thorns were added.

The thorns probably came from the jujube (*Ziziphus rhamnus christi*).

Just such a crown, dating to antiquity, is in the archives at Notre Dame de Paris.

10
CACTI AND BROMELIADS

What Are Succulents?

Although cacti, those strange-looking, prickly plants we associate with deserts, actually belong to several families, we group them (with numerous other plants) under the somewhat stranger heading of succulents.

Does that mean that they are sweet, tasty, and good to eat? Not at all. The term comes from the Latin *succulentis*, which means fleshy or juicy. Cactus are just one of many in the grouping. More than 30 plant families are included. The grouping has been made as much for convenience as anything.

Because most members are drought-resistant, dry-weather plants, the word describes them perfectly.

Plants qualifying as succulents can be found across a wide spectrum of the plant kingdom. Some are members of the amaryllis and lily families. Succulents even lurk among the daisies, and a couple of species among the geranium family qualify.

Included in the list are the tropical Bermuda, or Easter, lily and a plant few people think about—the asparagus.

As a category, these plants are called *xerophytes*, a Greek word that simply means "dry plants" and basically refers to desert-dwellers.

But not all succulents are desert-dwellers. Some rather unusual ones can be found in the heart of Central American rain forests.

How could these qualify? Even though their world is humid and rainy, the plants are tree-dwellers and use very little of the moisture. Rooted in tiny plots of moss and bits of bark, they remain essentially dry.

Amaryllis

While it may seem far-fetched, the beautiful and graceful amaryllis that blooms on many a window ledge has a very well known succulent for a relative—the century plant (*Agave americana*).

It is a member of the genus *Agave*, which includes more than 300 species.

Century Plant

Contrary to legend, century plants do not bloom once every hundred years. Most can come to flower in 10 to 50 years. But once they bloom, the tall portion dies, leaving behind numerous offshoots clustered about the base.

These make excellent container plants since they remain relatively small for years.

Lily Family

In the lily family, the most important succulents are those of the genus *Aloe*. Mostly natives of South Africa, they resemble the American *Agave*, but they are not related.

Aloe plants were known to early Greeks and Romans. Their resinous juice was often dispensed as a laxative.

Today the juice of *Aloe vera* is used to help heal burns. Many experts swear by it.

LEFT: *Surprisingly,* Agave ocahus, *shown here, belongs to the same family as the amaryllis and the century plant. In the* Agave *family, more than 300 species can be found from the south-western United States to the equator. The tough fibres of some species are used to produce sisal, a component in rope. The milky sap from others is used in making* pulque, *a powerful, rough-tasting, fast-acting Mexican drink.* RIGHT: *Among hobbyists, the best-known barrel cactus is this one, the golden barrel. It is shown here in its flowering stage.*

First Cacti

Paleobotanists believe that the first cacti evolved nearly 50 million years ago, when a hundred nameless seas covered what are now our deserts.

As the water receded, the earth changed and with it the climate was altered as well. A permanent belt of high-atmospheric pressure developed on each side of the equator, preventing the formation of rain. Weather still functions this way.

Plants caught in this strange, dry world were forced to develop methods of surviving on land with little rain.

They slowed their growth, changed their branch and leaf structure, and did other things. The more they changed, the more specialized they became.

Some plants became compact, shortening their leaves and stems to offer less surface for evaporation.

Others grouped their leaves in clusters, sometimes overlapping them like shingles on a roof, to protect them against the drying sun and wind.

To control evaporation, most cacti reduced the number of pores, or *stomata*, on their leaves. While one geranium leaf may contain as many as two million pores, many cacti reduced both the size and number by more than half.

Still others reduced the size or number of their leaves. On some plants, the dry spines we see are the remains of former leaves. Since many cacti would be tempting food for other desert-dwellers, the spines they've developed not only reduce evaporation but also provide excellent protection against predators.

To take advantage of this built-in protection, some birds find room within the spines for their nests and certain parasitic plants find a way of growing there.

Other varieties of cacti have created repulsive-tasting juices for protection. The *Dudleya* has a bitter, quinine-flavored juice that animals avoid.

Some plants solved the problem of evaporation by "lying low," virtually burying themselves in the sand.

Whatever combination of processes these plants devised, it was the hardiest that survived, permanently altered by the land and weather.

A Common Fallacy

Surprisingly, many people believe that a cactus can live without water. It cannot. Even the hardiest and "driest" of desert plants must have a reasonable amount.

This fact is borne out in the extremes of the Sahara Desert, where nothing survives. There is just too little rain.

What Makes Cactus Different?

All plants store some water in their roots, so water storage is a relative thing.

What makes cacti different from other plants is their unusual ability to store and protect quantities of water against loss for much longer periods. The procedure is so highly developed that no other plants can match it.

While some species developed thinner, tougher, drier stems to combat searing temperatures and dry conditions, most succulents moved in the opposite direction: They evolved special, thicker parts to provide water storage.

Some plants developed fleshy leaves; others created fleshier stems. Most cacti belong to the second group. With them, the stem was enlarged to provide increased water storage and to take over the vital functions of photosynthesis.

Though succulents can be found in many places, the cacti family is native to both American continents. Cacti have been found from the Arctic Circle in the north to Patagonia in the south.

Cacti were unknown in Europe before the Spaniards landed in the New World. The first mention of cactus came in 1540, when Coronado wrote about them in his reports.

In the deserts of North America, one sees a variety of land-based species, plants that are considered typical.

Yet further south, in the Caribbean and in tropical Central America, land-based varieties give way to strange tree-dwelling cacti.

Why Conserve Water?

Many desert species receive a full year's supply of water in less than one day, sometimes in a single rainfall. If you consider that the amount is the same as many tropical plants use up in a single day, you can understand why a desert plant has to conserve.

In many dry areas, rain comes but once a year and, in unusually dry times, plants may be forced to go two or three years without it.

Water-Saving Tricks

One way cacti conserve moisture is by producing a thick, sticky sap. Its very consistency reduces the rate of evaporation.

About one half of the species produces a normal, somewhat watery sap, while the other half produces a thicker, milkier sap.

A species called "noon flower" utilizes a series of unusual valves that can be closed to conserve water. This plant can survive up to three years without rain.

Some species even produce a chemical that binds with water to reduce evaporation.

The Great Cactus Show

The Mexican desert, especially areas just below the border with the United States, offers the world's greatest display of cactus.

One, organ pipe (*Lemaireocereus*), can reach a height of 20 feet. A version that's common in Arizona has rounded ribs and brown-to-purple spines.

Another, the barrel cactus (*Ferocactus*), is one of the best known, possibly for the not-so-accurate belief that if all else fails, one can get water from this source. (One can, but only as a moist pulp.)

The Mexicans have discovered two much more practical uses for the barrel cactus. They make fishhooks from the spines and a rather insipid "cactus candy" that attracts tourists by the droves.

Legend has it that the barrel cactus is known as the "compass plant" because it always tilts to the southeast. So reliable is this said to be that desert travellers use these plants as guides.

LEFT: *A native of Argentina,* Trichocereus candicans var. Robustior *is a member of a cacti family almost everyone recognizes, the organ pipe. Cactus hobbyists sometimes use this plant as grafting stock for other varieties.* RIGHT: Echinocereus dubious *is found in Texas.*

Climbing Cactus

There are even vinelike cacti, plants that reach out and up, like ivy.

The most spectacular is a relative of the night-blooming cereus: *Selenicereus macdonaldiae*. In some places it is known as the "queen of the night"—and with good reason. For sheer spectacle, no cactus can match its gold-and-white blossoms that are often a foot in diameter. Aerial roots support the plant as it climbs.

A list of other climbers would include *Aporocactus flagelliformis* (rattail), which can reach a height of three feet, and *Hylocereus undatus*, which is often cultivated for its fruit and, in Hawaii, is even used for hedges.

A Strange Succulent

Perhaps the most novel of all succulents (although not a cactus) is a tiny South African genus with just one plant, *Boweia volubilis*.

About 8 inches in diameter, the plant grows half-buried and each year produces long, thin, twisting stems that some say resemble "ornamental asparagus."

The plant is so rugged, so used to growing with little water that it has even been known to bloom without soil on a museum shelf after four years of storage.

Meet the Bromeliad

If you say nothing else about these plants, you can say that they belong to a large and strange family whose varieties are mostly limited to the tropical parts of the American continents. (There is one exception, a species quite unexpectedly found in West Africa.)

Highly decorative, they've been used as house plants for nearly a century.

They are mostly *epiphytic;* that is, they usually need another plant for support although not necessarily for food.

More than 2,000 species have been identified.

While their most common support is trees and shrubs, some bromeliads grow on the ground and a few grow on rocks. A handful have been found growing on cactus, where they use the spines of the host for protection.

These plants do not rely on their roots for nourishment but more as an anchor. The center of the plant, a rosettelike shape, forms a cup. Most species live on whatever food and moisture falls into this cup and on what can be absorbed through special scales on their leaves.

Sometimes a desert-based bromeliad has a mutual-aid arrangement with a desert frog. The amphibian, which needs moisture, lives in the always damp cup. It could not otherwise survive in such a hostile environment.

Scales on the plant absorb whatever mineral content and moisture there is in the air, passing it along to the leaves.

In rain forests, where moisture is no problem, the scales are missing and the plants absorb moisture in a more normal fashion.

Explaining the Names

These plants are found in two families. One is *Bromelia*, named for Olaf Bromel, a Swedish botanist. The other is *Tillandsia*, in honor of the Swedish physician Elias Tillands.

Tillandsia is an example of a botanical joke. Most plants in the group are desert-dwellers, used to living in a dry climate far from any water. Elias Tillands, as the botanist who named the plants knew, absolutely hated water. It was all his family could do to get him to cross a river.

Useful Bromeliads

While most plants in the bromeliad family are grown for decorative purposes, some are extremely useful in their native lands.

A few are used to make vinegar. Others are converted to juice and used to flavor a popular soft drink.

The fibres of others are used to make rope and, in Brazil, one species, a false pineapple, has a netlike fibre that is harvested to make fishnets.

Best-Known Bromeliads

If you go by name alone, "bromeliads" sounds formidable, but at least two are very familiar.

The first is Spanish moss (*Tillandsia usneoides*), which is neither Spanish nor a moss. In the United States, it is common throughout the South, where it can be found growing on trees.

The other is the pineapple. It can be found fresh in most supermarkets and canned in many homes.

More about Bromeliads

Most plants in the group have swordlike leaves in rosette form and unusual scales, which create a remarkable system for absorbing essential moisture and minerals.

Their water demands vary. While some cannot live without frequent rains, a handful has not seen moisture other than fog for years. Some live in the hottest deserts; others live high in the coldest elevations of the Andes. But the greatest variety is found in the rain forests of eastern Brazil.

The Pineapple

Columbus discovered the first bromeliad, the pineapple (*Ananas ssp.*), on his second voyage in 1493. The discovery was made on the West Indian island of Guadeloupe.

The pineapple's botanical name, *Annas*, is derived from the word the Guarani Indians of Brazil used to designate the species.

Even in the time of Columbus, the pineapple was a cultivated crop. Natives maintained groves and regularly harvested the fruit.

The fruit was so delicious that the explorer carried it back to Queen Isabella and it became so popular that the demand quickly outstripped the supply.

The first known picture of a pineapple appeared in 1535 in a book titled *The Universal History of India*. (If the title seems confusing, "India" referred to the New World, the Western Hemisphere, which Columbus had discovered. Originally, Europeans thought it was India.)

First attempts to cultivate the pineapple in Europe were made in 1690, when the plant was introduced in England. Within a year or two, growers were testing groves in Brussels.

Today, it is a profitable commercial crop in many tropical countries.

The common commercial plant is generally *Ananas comosus*, also known as "smooth cayenne," not because it has a strong peppery taste, but because Cayenne is the name of the town from which the plant came.

The smallest pineapple, a tiny dwarf, *Ananas nana*, is so little that it can be grown in a 4 inch pot. The fruit is seldom more than an inch or two in length.

One of the largest, *Ananas bracteatus*, has leaves 5 feet in length.

Perching Plants

One spectacular bromeliad, more than 3 feet in diameter, with a tall, dramatic spike and watermelon-colored bracts, lives high above the ground, perched comfortably on the branches of tall trees. Not a dry-land plant, it prefers a dense, hot environment.

Because it is found so far above ground, perched so high in the sky, it was given the unusual but suitable name of *Aechmea Mariae Reginae*, which means "Mary, Queen of Heaven."

It is used to decorate churches and to add color to certain religious celebrations in its homeland of Costa Rica.

───── 11 ─────
HOW PLANTS "TALK,"
"THINK," AND "TRAVEL"

Plant Responses

A recent study, conducted by an official U.S. laboratory in Maryland, indicates that plants are more responsive to human thoughts and talk than we suspected. By attaching a lie detector, or polygraph, to the leaves, one researcher proved that a plant can respond to various stimuli.

In one test, even thoughts of harm (by the researcher) could make the needle jump, indicating that the plant perceived a threat and reacted.

Plant "Talk"

Believing that plants can understand the human voice, an expert with the Japanese police also wired a cactus to a polygraph. The machine had been previously modified so that it could record the human voice, indicating the vocal range on a graph.

In this test, the man reversed the procedure, recording the plant's reactions and transforming them into sounds. The process, according to one reporter, gave the cactus an electronic "voice."

Before the test was over, the plant was responding to conversation through a series of audible electronic "hums." It was found to react to a number of pleasant and promising situations.

Since the initial test, the plant has been exhibited throughout Japan, where audiences swear it "talks."

"At times," the man told one audience, "the plant seems almost jolly."

Can Plants "Feel" Things?

Although certain tests have been questioned, a number of researchers in the United States and the Soviet Union have insisted that they have recorded "meaningful" plant vibrations: specific plant reactions to specific situations.

At the University of California at Davis, one researcher recorded the response of plants to a number of stressful situations—a lack of water, having a leaf cut, being given water, and more. In every case, the plant emitted a specific electronic response that could be both differentiated from other responses and measured.

By converting the signals into sounds, the researcher created what some have called "plant talk"—although no one has yet held a conversation with a carnation.

Talking to Plants

Luther Burbank, known as the American "wizard of horticulture," had similar ideas. He believed that, like humans, plants have sensory perceptions. He once listed 20 plantlike responses.

"I talk to plants to create vibrations of love," he said.

It's All in the Tip

More than one botanist has suggested that plants can somehow "think" because, no matter how haphazardly one plants them, the roots always grow down, while the stem rises majestically above the surface of the ground—even when the seed is reversed.

In 1880 Charles Darwin demonstrated that it was no accident, by proving that the part of the plant that controlled this aspect of growth was located a short distance behind the root tip.

By removing this segment, Darwin made it clear that without it, a plant had no idea of where it was growing. With it attached, a plant reacted as plant life should.

He proved that something found here could sense gravity, sending growing instructions to the rest of the plant.

Responding to Light

For years scientists believed that the element that controlled the direction of root and stem growth was either an electrical charge or an unrecorded "irritation," a jolt of "something" that somehow caused a "directional" response.

The real answer surfaced when botanists began experimenting with chemistry, studying how plants respond to light.

Most gardeners remember that a plant follows light. Wherever it is planted, it turns in the direction of the sun.

Tests have shown that when light was moved, the plant growth followed, the plant always bent to grow in the direction of the light.

But when the tip was removed, this bending did not occur. The plant no longer followed light.

Science has given this unusual bending action a special name: *tropism*. It is derived from a Greek word meaning "to turn."

A number of independent tests in several countries have proved that it was neither an electrical charge nor a nervous impulse that caused the response.

The action was the result of an amazing family of chemical substances that scientists call *auxins* (from the Greek word *auxe*, meaning "to increase"). Auxins are responsive to light.

Each part of a plant requires a different auxin level.

As a general rule, the area with the most auxin grows the fastest.

If light is equal on all sides of an erect stem, the amount of auxins will be even and growth will continue normally.

But if light comes from only one side, auxins on the lighted side are destroyed, made less effective, or transferred to the shaded side. In response, the darker side grows, elongates, and bends.

A plant's urge to reach light is called *phototropism*.

Amazing Auxin

Scientists still do not completely understand the manner in which the chemical works, but recent studies have given us more information.

Auxin is found in the stem, root tips, and other parts of plants. Surprisingly little is required. It is continuously produced in minute amounts. In addition to sensing direction, it is responsible for the way in which plants "travel" and climb.

A Gardening Trick Explained

Gardeners have made use of this knowledge for centuries, although they may not have been able to explain it in technical terms.

While auxin levels vary in different parts of a plant, too much—at any point—inhibits growth.

If a plant's normal balance is upset by removing the leader (the main point of growth and the source of auxin in a specific area), the level is lowered.

Lateral stems suddenly grow and buds, if there are any, may open.

Gardeners far back into history have used this system, pinching back the tips of such plants as chrysanthemum to stimulate bushier branches.

How Do Roots Grow Down?

Although auxins control directional growth, chemistry alone doesn't fully explain how roots "know" how to grow down or the stem to grow up. What governs that? Gravity. It causes heavier things to descend and lighter things to rise.

Often when a stem breaks through the ground, it seems at first to be growing horizontally. Suddenly it changes direction, springing upright. Why? Again auxins are responsible. They accumulate or become less active on the lower side. This stimulates growth, which turns the plant upright.

In the case of roots, we suspect that gravity "pulls" auxins to the lower side. Growth in the upper portion is encouraged, which bends the root downwards.

Tricky Climbers

Most climbing plants were originally woodland species. The woodlands were shaded and the plants required more light than was available. Their answer to this dilemma was to climb above the shaded forest floor. To accomplish this, they had to rely on trees and bushes for support.

Climbers are essentially travelling plants, species that have discovered ways to move.

They've devised a number of surprising methods: the creation of tendrils that grow from a stem, leaf, or even the flower; the use of adhesive pads and holdfasts; and the most direct approach, by twining and curling. A few plants even hang on through the use of sharp thorns.

Climbing plants have devised a number of methods of "travelling," including the creation of tendrils that grow from the stem, as shown here. In the picture on the left, we see the tendril developing from the stem and then, in the one on the right, we see it twining and attaching to another plant for support.

Such plants as ivy and Virginia creeper rely on adhesive pads. Ivy uses aerial roots with attached pads; the creeper settles for pads alone.

Plants with pads can find a safe haven on the steepest walls. You see them growing on the sides of old houses, over high fences, and up tall trees.

"Sensing" Climbers

One type of climber seems to use a muscular reaction much like that of our fingers. Actually these devices are octopuslike tendrils, long stems or stalks without leaves, which twine around a tree or fence in an upward serpentine spiral.

As they grow, they "sense" the surface and keep searching until they find what seems like a promising support.

At that point, the cells on one side grow with an amazing burst of speed, while those on the other side remain stationary and unchanged. As a result, the tip curls rapidly and, in short order, the plant has a new hold.

There is no established pattern. Some plants spiral in a clockwise direction; others turn counterclockwise.

Wisteria and summer jasmine are examples.

Many clematises use a similar system but, lacking specialized tendrils, must twist their main stems, those with leaves.

Fastest Climber?

What is the most vigorous climber? No one keeps records, but a safe guess would be *Actinida chinensis*, one of a family of 40 or so climbing shrubs discovered more than a hundred years ago in Asia. It can reach a height of 30 feet.

A close relative, *A. kolomikta* is better known to gardeners because it is less vigorous, normally reaching heights of less than 12 feet. It is very popular in Japan, where it is known as "cat's medicine."

Cat's Medicine

Why is it called "cat's medicine"? Because it is thought to affect cats more noticeably than either catnip or valerian.

In ancient Japan, it was said that if charcoal makers burned wood wrapped in this vine, cats would come from miles around to congregate around the fire, eventually rolling on the ground as if they were intoxicated.

Tallest Ferns

While most of the ferns that grow in North America are low-growing woodland varieties, in some parts of the world they tower high enough to dominate the skyline.

Tropical tree ferns, whose stems resemble palm trees, reach heights of 50 feet, which makes them tall enough to surpass some true trees. With fronds 6 feet or more in length, they were thought to be trees by early explorers.

What Exactly Is a Fern?

Some consider a fern a prehistoric flower and, in a way, they aren't far off.

What passes for the stalk on more complex plants is normally hidden beneath the ground on a fern.

Roots grow from this stemlike portion.

The segments you see above ground are called "fronds." They are "true" leaves.

Spores, the manner by which ferns reproduce, are shed directly from the leaf.

It is not surprising that early botanists did not immediately recognize that the almost invisible spores are the reproductive element, because they are part of a two-phase process.

The spores do not create a new plant but become a flat thallus, from which a new generation of fern ultimately grows.

The ancient Greeks believed that since the spores were nearly invisible, the quality could be transferred. They insisted that if they ate some, they too would become invisible.

Fern Leaves

Flowering plants, which in the evolutionary cycle followed ferns, lost something in the transformation.

Fern leaves are more versatile than those of flowers. For a period of time, as fern leaves form, they continue to grow at their tips.

The tip is coiled and inside there is, for a short time, something miraculous called an *apical meristem*, "botanese" for an unusual kind of cellular tissue (the stuff from which plants are made) that has not yet undergone a change. For a brief time, it literally has the choice of becoming a leaf or a root.

No latter-day leaf can duplicate that trick.

The Walking Fern

The fern that best illustrates this ability is the walking fern *Camptosorus rhizophyllis*, an evergreen found in lime-rock areas of North America.

Fern leaves are more versatile than those of comparable flowers. As the leaves form, they continue to grow at their tips and the tips themselves coil. For a brief time, they become a miraculous kind of form, an apical meristem, which means that they have an unusual kind of cellular tissue that has not yet undergone change. At this point, they have the choice of becoming either a leaf or a root.

While it does not look much like a true fern, some of its leaves develop familiar threadlike tips. When one of them touches moist moss or earth, new leaves and roots develop.

Soon they are joined to the parent plant, which is some distance away, by nothing more than a small part of the old leaf. In time this part separates and the plant stands by itself.

As the process is repeated, small pieces of the original plant move surprising distances from their original "home."

It is this trick that gave the plant its name.

Ancestors of Flowers

Millions of years ago, before true flowers evolved, much of the land was covered with ferns very similar to those we've been discussing.

How did flowers develop? While most ferns reproduce through the use of spores, experts think that in some cases ancient spores evolved into seeds (which were produced at the edges of their fronds).

It is these prehistoric seeds, long since passed from sight, that are the ancestors of the flowering plants we see around us.

Travelling Plants

In our time very few plants are limited to the region in which they originally evolved. Many have expanded their territory well beyond their homeland because their seeds were carried by birds and animals. Others were transplanted by humans.

Species growing away from their original home are said to have been "naturalized."

Almond trees are associated with the Mediterranean coast because they seem to have been there forever. In reality, they were brought to the area centuries ago by early travellers. Their original homeland is the Middle East.

The citrus family has a similar history. Though well distributed throughout the world, citrus trees originated in Southeast Asia.

The pasqueflower (*Pulsatilla vulgaris*) was given its name because it flowers around Easter. Botanists believe that it was introduced to England by Roman soldiers.

LEFT: *Azalea blossoms. Although azaleas and rhododendrons are found in many places, they are essentially Oriental plants. In the seventeenth and eighteenth centuries, when European trade with Japan began, many plants were introduced to Europe. In America, native azaleas are found along a 2,000-mile stretch of the Atlantic and Gulf plains, roughly from Maine to Texas and the Appalachian Mountain range. Native American varieties were discovered by English missionaries from 1690 on.* RIGHT: *Foxglove* (Digitalis purpurea), *a member of the figwort family, was brought to the United States from Europe for garden use and then "escaped" to become so common in the wild that it is now confused with native plants. One frequently sees it growing along highways in California, Oregon, and Washington. It is well known for the drug it yields, digitalis, named for the plant and commonly prescribed as a heart stimulant.*

12
MORE UNUSUAL FACTS

Miraculous Machinery

If we could describe a plant in no other way, we might say that it is a highly efficient machine, so complex that it's little short of miraculous. Consider the transportation of sap, the life-giving fluid of all plants. No one quite knows how the movement works, although scientists have a pretty good idea in a general sense. That aside, a plant can "pull" food in liquid form from its roots to its growing fruit at the rate of several inches an hour.

No man-made system of hydraulic plumbing can match it. Scientists speak in terms of root pressures, osmosis, transpiration, and more, yet the details remain a substantial mystery.

Transpiration

In botany, the term describes the process of giving off vapors (as liquid and as gaseous liquids) through the stomata, or pores, of a plant. It is an important element of plant life.

A grass plant can transpire its weight in water every day.

A stalk of corn can vaporize more than a gallon of water every day. It has been estimated that a corn plant loses over 50 gallons of water during a full growing season.

In a cornfield that would add up to enough water to cover the field at a depth of more than a foot.

On a one-acre farm, corn would run through the equivalent of 350,000 gallons of water every year.

An apple tree can transpire more than 2,000 gallons in a single season.

Lunar Power

For centuries man has believed that the moon has a direct effect on gardening and plant growth.

In *Historia Naturalis*, a 37-volume encyclopedia of natural science published about the time of Christ, Pliny the Elder made a number of suggestions to Roman gardeners based on the effects of moon phases.

For juicy, elegant-looking fruit and vegetables, Pliny suggested picking crops during a full moon "at a time when ants were busiest," even though that meant working at night.

That was the prime time to harvest oysters as well, he said, since they were in their period of fastest growth.

On the other hand, Pliny said that during a new moon, while ants and oysters were listless, fruit was less susceptible to rotting. If it was to be dried, he believed, it would preserve better if picked at that time.

Carnivorous Plants

Despite the obvious dedication of vegetarians to eating plants, the truth is that a surprising number of plants themselves are devoted to eating meat. One hundred or more plants are every bit as interested in a square meal of flesh as any lion or tiger.

Botanists believe that these plants, mostly dwellers in bogs and marshes, developed their habits because the earth where they lived was deficient in certain amino acids. So, the plants devised several unique ways of attracting and trapping insects.

A large number are known as "pitcher plants." The name derives from these plants having developed a trap that utilizes special leaves that hold moisture like a pitcher or gourd.

The trap allows an insect to enter but, once in, keeps it from withdrawing.

In many, the trap has literally become a primitive stomach, capable of digesting the insect it captures.

One Carnivorous Plant: The Cobra Lily

In the United States the best-known plant-family carnivore is the cobra lily (*Darlingtonia californica*), found in northern California and southern Oregon. The cobra lily has a hooded head and a forked "tongue" (called a "fishtail"), which resemble a colorfully spotted snake.

The roof of the hood, or dome, is covered with windows that are almost glasslike in their transparency. These illuminate the interior, give an illusion of "freedom," and help trap food.

The pitcher and the tongue are covered with a nectar that lures many kinds of insect. Ants are attracted from ground level and flying insects drop in from the sky.

Once they enter the hooded area, escape is rare. The obvious route seems to lead to the top, or windowed area, but if insects fly to the ceiling, they slip, lose their footing, and drop into the pitcher. Once their wings are moistened by the water in the bottom, they rarely escape.

The Amazing Water Lily

Can you name the world's fastest-growing plant? No one knows for certain, but if you said the giant water lily (*Victoria amazonica*), you'd be close. Found only in the Amazon basin, it can develop from seed to full size—a huge plant with 6-foot circular leaves—in just seven months.

And Bamboo, Too

Another fast-growing plant, perhaps the true record-holder, is bamboo.

In England, *Bamboo vulgaris* has been known to grow some 40 feet in just 40 days.

In California, 30 inches of growth has been recorded in 24 hours.

Asparagus Bracts

While flowering plants consist of three components—roots, stem, and leaves—the leaf on some plants may not look like one.

On the common asparagus (*Asperagus officinalis*), as on similax, a nonedible version of the same plant used by florists, the stem is predominant. The leaves are inconspicuous protrusions, woody bumps known as "bracts." Botanists define bracts as "much reduced leaves."

Incidentally, the plant can be grown from seed, although commercial crops are most often created from year-old thinned and transplanted crowns.

Stalks are normally green. "White" asparagus, especially popular in Europe, is created during farming. The stalks are blanched, or whitened, by hilling soil over the row and then harvesting it beneath the ground with special tools.

Cacti Are Also Different

The outer layer of cacti, the portion that resembles a stem, contains chlorophyll and functions as leaves do.

The bulk of the stem tissue is devoted to the storage of moisture, almost like a tank. It is this adaptation that allows cacti to survive so long in dry, rainless deserts.

Plant Foods

While good gardeners nurture their plants with fertilizers, minerals, and chemical additives, these are not plant foods. They are merely the beginning.

The elements in them may be essential to the development of plants, but the components that plants consider to be food (directly or via conversion) are the same as those used by humans: sugar, starch, fat, and protein.

LEFT: Opuntia phaecantha, *common in southern California deserts.* RIGHT: Trichocereus grandiflora *is a native of Argentina.*

Amazing Photosynthesis

If any of nature's processes seem so complex as to be virtually unbelievable, the prime example, a major miracle in itself, must be *photosynthesis*—the procedure by which plants convert an inedible substance into nutritious, useful food.

The process takes place in the leaves and begins with the tiny "green" units called *chloroplasts*. These are found in the plant's leaf cells. The word comes to us from the Greek in two parts: *chloro*, meaning "green," and *plast*, meaning "that which forms."

The colored material itself is called *chlorophyll*, which means "green leaf." A plant uses two types of chlorophyll, which are different yet similar components.

The process begins with glucose, a sugar readily available in leaves. A plant cannot directly digest or utilize the sugar. To be of use, sugar must be converted to starch.

The conversion cannot be accomplished without sunlight. The sun provides the energy. It penetrates the leaf's upper layers, those richest in chlorophyll. The process works in the following manner.

All chemicals consist of individual units called molecules. Each type of chemical has a special arrangement. For the plant's purposes, the molecular structures of glucose (an unusable sugar) and starch (which can be used) are so close that only a few molecules need to be rearranged to convert one to the other.

Working as a team, sunlight and chlorophyll take the glucose molecules and shuffle them around. The result: a highly nutritious starch.

Incidentally, the "green" part of a plant is one of the most important elements for mankind. All of the world's food not produced from synthetics begins in the green parts of plants, either directly, as in the grain we eat, or indirectly, as when we feed grain to cattle.

Without Chlorophyll

As we've seen, plants with chlorophyll can produce their own food.

Without it, plants must either find another process, create a substitute food, or live off the work of those that have it.

A large number of species lacking chlorophyll sponge off the varieties that do. The spongee is called the host; the sponger is a parasite.

A parasite does none of the work while enjoying all of the benefits.

An example known to almost everyone is mistletoe. Although it has chlorophyll, it does not live by its own efforts. It generally finds a home on the higher branches of trees, commonly on oaks, where it attaches itself by means of an *haustoria*. The word comes from Latin and means "sucking mouth." Utilizing this device, mistletoe breaks through the bark and absorbs life-giving fluid directly from the host tree.

Fungi

An extremely large family of primitive parasitic plants, fungi include mushrooms, fungus, and mould. The exact number in the family is unknown, although experts believe that there are more than 100,000.

You could say that fungi are restless travellers. Reproductive spores move in clouds above the earth and there is no part of the planet without some version of them.

Many experts believe that fungoid forms are as old as rooted plants. Some insist they are much older.

Early Greek writers had a poor opinion of mushrooms and other fungi. More than one insisted that they grew "among rusty nails and serpents' lairs," which was not true. The same writers thought that an association with rust and serpents' fangs explained why some mushrooms are poisonous.

Lacking chlorophyll, fungi are dependent on other plants for their carbohydrates and nitrogen. These essential elements are obtained in two ways: first, in the manner of mistletoe, from living organisms, and second, from decaying remains.

An ability to secrete a number of enzymes allows them to digest components that other plants cannot make use of.

Because of this feature, many fungi are extremely beneficial, speeding along and promoting nature's process of decay. In short, hardworking fungi help to clean our planet.

Fungi are also important in areas of medicine. An example that we're all familiar with is penicillin. Another is ergot, an important drug used in obstetrics. It is obtained from the mould *Claviceps purpurea*.

Oldest Mushroom

The world's oldest mushroom, a speck of life more than 40 million years in age, was discovered recently by a University of California researcher in the Dominican Republic.

Growing on an ancient tree, it had been covered with resin. The accident had preserved it for the ages. When found, it had been preserved in the middle of a piece of ancient amber.

Identified by specialists at the Field Museum of Natural History in Chicago, it was determined to be a new and unknown species and was given a special scientific name, *Coprinites dominicana*, to honor the republic where it was found.

Fungal Symbiosis

"Symbiosis" means the living together of dissimilar organisms in a manner that is mutually beneficial.

The process is common enough in nature. In the fungi family, a classic example is found in lichen, which joins in mutual assistance with an alga.

The alga receives water and essential organic substances and, in some cases, is protected against drying out.

The lichen, which is the dominant partner, derives its essential food from the alga, sometimes directly through a sucking attachment.

LEFT: Polyporus versicolor. *Found on dead and decaying trees, these fungi quicken the pace of reforestation. Polypores are a different type of fungi with tubes and pores in place of the gills seen so often. Many species grow to substantial sizes and can live for years.* RIGHT: *Lichen.*

Gourmet Mushrooms

A number of mushrooms are edible and some are highly prized by gourmets.

Morels are popular in France and truffles, found underground, are among the world's most rare and expensive foods. They provide a delicate flavoring in some of the world's most prized recipes.

A number of mushrooms are grown commercially. The shitake, popular in the Orient, has recently been imported.

Poisonous Mushrooms

Not all mushrooms are edible. A number are poisonous to some degree or another. One of the most dangerous is the *Amanita muscara*, the Fly Agaric or Angel of Death. It can kill in a matter of hours.

Because of the dangers of some, one should never hunt mushrooms for table use without expert assistance.

Banana

Although bananas are usually associated with Central America, they originated in Asia. They were introduced to the New World from the Canary

Islands, brought there by Father de Berenga, a friend of Columbus and the same Catholic missionary who concluded that plants were designed exactly the same as humans—only inside out.

Most of us would say that bananas grow on trees, but we'd be wrong. Springing from an underground rhizome, much like such flowers as the iris, the banana is a giant herb.

The portion above ground is a false trunk. The fruit develops from yellowish flowers.

Each banana plant produces 50 to 100 bananas.

A single bunch can weigh between 50 and 125 pounds, just about the limit that a strong man can comfortably carry.

Currently more than 100 varieties are in cultivation.

Valuable Crocus

One crocus, *Crocus sativus*, a member of the family *Iridacaea* (which includes the iris), may be the most profitable of all garden plants.

One small part of it, the stigma and a portion of the style, is used to make saffron.

The part used is so small that it has been estimated that 4,000 stigmata are required to make one ounce of saffron. Little wonder that it is so rare and costly.

The Moors introduced it to Spain in about 961 A.D. Cultivated for

A species of common wood-lover often found under fallen trees.

centuries in Persia, it is a popular and costly ingredient still used in many ways.

In earlier times it was used in medicines. It is mentioned in a tenth-century doctor's handbook. It was a popular ingredient in salves.

Strewn along the streets when Nero made his entry into Rome, saffron scented his route.

One major use was as a dye. Saffron yellow was a royal color in early Greece.

Today saffron is used in the United States and Europe to add flavoring and color to rice. It is an essential ingredient in the popular Spanish dish *paella*.

It is currently grown in Spain and parts of France and Sicily as well as in some areas of the Middle East.

The true crocus should not be confused with the autumn crocus, which, though it has a similar name, is related to the lily.

Lavender

In the Middle Ages, lavender was considered the most valuable of all perfumes. Then, as now, it was used to scent bath water.

In the sixteenth century, doctors believed that it was an effective medication against the loss of speech.

In Culpeper's *Herbal*, the author swore it cured headaches.

The Willow

In 1763 an English preacher, Edward Stone, made an unexpected connection: He realized that willows were likely to flourish in marshy regions where rheumatism was prevalent.

In his day it was a common theory that "like cured like" and, acting on that assumption, Stone made a decoction from willow bark.

In the decoction process, salicylic acid was discovered, a compound still effective in the relief of rheumatic pain. The name derives from *salix*, Latin for willow. The compound is found in a number of popular and effective over-the-counter pain relievers today.

Wormwood

For many people, the word "vermouth" suggests a popular drink, the ubiquitous martini. Few of us realize that it is actually a derivative of another term also connected with liquor—wormwood.

Wormwood is associated with absinthe, which calls to mind French Gay Nineties decadence. Still, *Artemisia absinthium* (wormwood) has long been known as a flavoring in drinks.

The gossipy Pliny said it was popular in Rome, as it was used to prevent fevers and to "generally improve one's health."

Travellers were told to carry a small amount, sampling it from time to time to avoid fatigue.

It was thought that the plant was discovered by the goddess Diana, who gave it to the founder of medicine, the centaur Chiron.

In Italy even after the Second World War, drivers were seen with sprigs in their cars to ward off evil.

LEFT: *Lavender* (Lavandula cv.) *(meaning the cultivated type) is common in Provence, France. "When distilled," said Dioscorides, "it surpasses all other perfumes." People practising magic have long used lavender in love potions and sachets. To make a love note especially potent, seventeenth-century women rubbed lavender onto the paper. If, as a gardener, you want to attract bees and butterflies, plant lavender. They love it.* RIGHT: *Wormwood* (Artemisia caucus). *A relative,* Artemisia absinthium, *is used to flavor the notorious alcoholic drink absinthe.*

Tea

Tea, the world's leading caffeine beverage, is a product of the leaves of one camellia: thea or *Camellia sinensis.*

The common name originates with *t'e,* a Chinese word (Amoy dialect) pronounced "tay." It was taken up by the Dutch and comes to us, changed to "tee," via England.

Chinese legend says that tea drinking began in about 2737 B.C. with a mythological emperor, Shen Nung.

According to another legend, the shrub originated when a Buddhist saint, Bodhidharma (or Daruma) fell asleep during his devotions. On awakening, he cut off his eyelids and threw them on the ground. Where they fell, a bush appeared. Its leaves, infused in water, created a liquid that prevented sleep.

The plant was originally grown in Southeast Asia. Its use spread as Buddhism saw the consumption of tea as a means of combating intemperance.

On Rooftops

One of several plants known as hen-and-chickens, houseleek (*Sempervivum soboliferum*) has an unusual history. In earlier times it was grown in the most unexpected of places—on rooftops.

Raised mostly because it was thought to be lucky, it also helped to seal and waterproof primitive homes.

Charlemagne, king of the Franks, made it a law that houseleeks had to be planted on every roof in his kingdom.

Houseleek was considered one of nature's best good-luck charms and, in Charlemagne's time, it was believed that the plant protected a house against strikes of lightning.

Grown between the roof tiles, it must have given houses of the time a strange, almost "fuzzy" appearance.

The Importance of Buds

Buds, an early signal of the growth of a stem or flower, are commercially important.

Cloves, used in most kitchens as a seasoning, are the dried, unopened buds of a tropical tree, *Eugenia aromatica*. It is a member of the myrtle family, a large group of popular trees and shrubs.

The globe artichoke (*Cynara scolymus*) is the bud or unopened flower of a plant related to the common thistle.

Largest Family

The largest family of garden flowers is *Compositae*, the composite or sunflower family. These flowers have been grouped together because they are "inflorescent." That means that the heads are clustered.

The category includes more than 20,000 species and 950 genera, or plant

LEFT: *Seaside daisy, or beach aster* (Erigeron glaucus), *commonly called fleabane, is a member of the* Compositae *genus, aster tribe. It is common to coastal areas of California and Oregon.* RIGHT: *Another daisy, a member of the genus* Compositae, *aster tribe.*

Ageratum, *known also as flossflower, is a member of the* Compositae *genus, eupatorium tribe.*

families. Included are many popular varieties such as asters, marigolds, and, or course, the sunflower.

The family is so large that botanists have added one dozen subdivisions to the listing. These are called tribes.

The aster tribe has more than 100 families and 2,000 species. One of the best known is the Michaelmas daisy.

The calendula tribe has 160 species. One of its best known flowers is the pot marigold.

When Flowers Don't Seem Like Flowers

Not all flowers are immediately recognizable as such. In some species, the flowers can be mistaken or overlooked completely. In a few, the sexual components have been divided so as to be almost unrecognizable. Corn is an example.

In corn, the "male" portion has been crowded into the long tassel.

The female segment forms the edible ear.

The female stigma is the "silk" that protrudes from the covering that protects the ear.

The Pineapple

Probably the most surprising adaptation of this kind is the pineapple. The fruit—the part we eat—is not really what we think it is. It is an example of "inflorescence," or a cluster of flowers.

The petals and stamens have fallen and the sepals and ovaries are crowded into one edible segment.

The part we normally consider a flower has been transformed.

You might expect to find seeds, but commercial varieties are raised without them.

And the Incredible Edible Fig

Another example one might never suspect is the fig. The juicy part we eat so happily is actually a cluster of flowers turned inside out.

Lining the inner surface are tiny flowers—female, male, and neutered.

The unit, called a *syconium*, is pollinated by a miniature wasp.

Metric Equivalents

INCHES TO MILLIMETRES AND CENTIMETRES

MM—millimetres   CM—centimetres

Inches	MM	CM	Inches	CM	Inches	CM
⅛	3	0.3	9	22.9	30	76.2
¼	6	0.6	10	25.4	31	78.7
⅜	10	1.0	11	27.9	32	81.3
½	13	1.3	12	30.5	33	83.8
⅝	16	1.6	13	33.0	34	86.4
¾	19	1.9	14	35.6	35	88.9
⅞	22	2.2	15	38.1	36	91.4
1	25	2.5	16	40.6	37	94.0
1¼	32	3.2	17	43.2	38	96.5
1½	38	3.8	18	45.7	39	99.1
1¾	44	4.4	19	48.3	40	101.6
2	51	5.1	20	50.8	41	104.1
2½	64	6.4	21	53.3	42	106.7
2	76	7.6	22	55.9	43	109.2
3½	89	8.9	23	58.4	44	111.8
4	102	10.2	24	61.0	45	114.3
4½	114	11.4	25	63.5	46	116.8
5	127	12.7	26	66.0	47	119.4
6	152	15.2	27	68.6	48	121.9
7	178	17.8	28	71.1	49	124.5
8	203	20.3	29	73.7	50	127.0

INDEX

bees, 14–15, 53–54
beetle flowers, 13
beetles, 47, 55
belladonna (*Atropa belladonna*; deadly
    nightshade), 70
belladonna lily (*Amaryllis belladonna*), 69
Berberis thunbergii (Japanese bayberry), 23
birds, 59
black bean, 29
black spruce (*Picea mariana*), 18
botanical names, 21, 22; descriptive terms of,
    25–28; religious meanings, 28–35
Bougainvillaea, 21
Boweia volubilis, 97
boxwood, 29, 79
Brassica oleracea (sea cabbage), 64
bristlecone pine (*Pinus aristata*), 18
Bromel, Olaf, 98
Bromelia, 98
bromeliads, 97–99
bucket orchid (*Coryanthes macrantha*), 13–14
buds, 118
bulrushes, 91
Burbank, Luther, 101
bush lupin (*Lupinus*), 30
buttercup family (*Ranunculus*), 26
butterfly flowers, 15
Buxus, 29
Buxus sempervirens (common box), 69

C

cabbage, 64
cactus, 92–95, 110; climbing, 97; first, 94;
    largest, 18; tree-sized, 18
calabash (*Lagenaria siceraria*), 20
Calendula officinalis (pot marigold), 27
Calluna vulgaris (Scotch heather), 49
camellia (*Camellia sinensis*; thea), 80, 117–118
Camptosorus rhizophyllis (walking fern), 105–106
Cannabinus l. (Indian hemp; bastard jute), 82
Capsella bursapastoris (shepherd's purse), 42
carbon dioxide, growth and, 43
Carboniferous period, 8, 17
cardon (*Pachycereus*), 18
Carex, 58
carnation, 29, 80
carnivorous plants, 109–110
castor beans, 68
cat's medicine, 104
cattail (*Typha latifolia*), 10
cedar, 29, 87
cedar of Lebanon (*Cedrus libam*), 87
Cedrus deodara, 29
Cedrus libani, 29
century plants, 93
Ceres chilensis (South American tree cactus), 43
Cereus giganteus (saguaro cactus), 18
Ceropegia, 53
Charlemagne, 60–61, 118
Chatham Island lily (*Myosotidium hortensis*), 79

chemical warfare, 42
Chinese evergreen, 29
Chinese hat (*Holmskioldia sanguinea*), 26
chlorophyll, 73, 111–112
chloroplasts, 111
Christmas cactus, 73
Christmas rose (*Helleborus niger*), 69
chrysanthemum, 26, 29, 73
Chrysanthemum frutescens (white marguerite), 33
Chrysanthemum maximum, 21
Chrysanthemum parthenium (feverfew), 63
Cirsium occidentale (western thistle), 23
citrus family, 107
Clark, Captain William, 24
Clarkai amoena (last-of-spring and summer
    darling), 24
clary sage (*Salvia sclarea*), 62
Claviceps purpurea, 113
clavus, 66
clematis, 80–81
Clematis montana, 80–81
climate, 16
climbers, 103–104
climbing cactus, 97
Clompositae, 33
clove (*Sygzygium aromaticum*), 66
cobra lily (*Darlingtonia californica*), 12, 109–110
coconut shell, 57
Colocasia esculenta, 42
color, importance of, 55
columbine, 29
common box (*Buxus sempervirens*), 69
common names, 21–22
compass plant, 96
Compositae, 72, 118–120
composite flower, 35
confection alkermes, 88
Conium maculatum (poisonous hemlock), 68
Convallaria majalis (lily-of-the-valley), 69
cookbooks, 61
Coprinities dominicana, 113
Coreopsis, 21
coriander (*Coriandrum sativum*), 26–27
cork oak, 88
corn, 44, 120
Cornus (dogwood), 29
Cornus florida (flowering dogwood), 89
Coryanthes macrantha (bucket orchid), 13–14
cotton, 90
cotyledons, 56
crest, 50
crocus, 29
Crocus sativus, 115–116
cross-fertilization, 47–48
crown imperial (*Fritillaria imperialis*), 24
Crown of Thorns (*Juncus balticus*), 91
Culpeper, Nicholas, 61–62
cultivated, plants; first, 20
cumin (*Umbelliferae cuminum*), 64–65
cup-and-saucer (*Holmskioldia sanguinea*), 26

Mondara didyma (scarlet bergamot), 63
mosquito plant (*Cynanchum acuminatifolium*), 52
mosses, 9–10
moth, yucca and, 50–51
moth flowers, 15
mountain ash, 86
mountain laurel (*Kalmia latifolia*), 52
mushrooms, 54; gourmet, 114; hallucinogenic, 68; oldest, 113; poisonous, 114
mustard seed, 33
"mycorrhizal" connection, 44
Myosotidium hortensis (Chatham Island lily), 79
myrtle, 33

N

names: from gods and legends, 24; of honor, 23
Narcissus poeticus, 77
Nelumbo (water lily), 32
nematodes, 40
nicotine, 41
night-blooming cereus (*Selenicereus macdonaldiae*), 97
noon flower, 96
nostrums, 61
Nymphaea (lotus), 32
Nymphae citrina, 47

O

Ocimum basilicum (basil), 62
Oenothera hooker (evening primrose), 24
oldest: living trees, 18; mushrooms, 113; plants, 9, 19; trees, 17
oleander, 33
olive, 33
Ophrys, 15
Ophrys speculum, 49–50
opium poppy (*Papaver somniferum*), 69–70
Opuntia phaecantha, 81, 111
orange, 34
orchids, 14, 74–75, 76–78
orchid seeds, 77
organ pipe (*Lemaireocereus*), 96
Origanum (marjoram), 67
Oswego tea plant, 63
ovary, 45
oxymel, 64

P

Pachycereus (cardon), 18
paella, 116
palm, 34
pansy, 34
Papaver somniferum (opium poppy), 69–70
Papaver ssp. (poppy), 57
parasites, 42
pasqueflower (*Pulsatilla vulgaris*), 107
passionflower (*passiflora*), 34, 83
"patented" plants, first, 20
peach blossom, 34
peanuts, 90
pear, 34

Pelargonium domesticum (Martha Washington geranium), 75
penicillium, 42
Pentstemon digitalis (beard tongue), 26
peony, 83
perching plants, 99
Persea americana (avocado), 25
petunia, 59
pfingrose, 83
Phallus impudicus, 54–55
phenolic acid, 42
Philodendron cordatum (heartleaf philodendron), 27
Phorandendron (mistletoe), 37, 68
photosynthesis, 111–112
phototropism, 102
Phrygilanthus mutabilis, 43
Picea mariana (black spruce), 18
pinch traps, 53
pine, 34
pineapple, 99, 120
Pinus aristata (bristlecone pine), 18
Pisona grandis, 41
pistil, 36, 45
pitcher plants, 109
pitfall traps, 53
plane tree, 84–85
plant diseases, 40
plant foods, 110–111
plant friends and enemies, 44
plant names. *see* names
plant responses, 100
plant talk, 100
plant terms, commonly used, 35–36
Pliny the Elder, 44, 65, 66, 109
poinsettia, 73
poisonous plants, 67–70
pollen, 36, 47; importance of, 46; saving, 48–49; types, 48
pollination, 47; by bats, 52; guaranteeing, 76–77; trapping mechanisms, 53
pollination bondage, 52
pollinators, 46
Polyporus versicolor, 114
Polystichum dudleyi (shield fern), 42
pomegranate, 34, 88–89
poppy seed (*Papaver*), 57
pot marigold (*Calendula officinalis*), 27
prairie grass, 90
preservation, of lettuce, 64
Pronuba yuccasella, 50
pseudocopulation, 50
Pulsatilla vulgaris (pasqueflower), 107
pussy willow, 34

Q

Quercus coccifera, 88

R

Ranunculus sp. (buttercup family), 26
rattail (*Aporocactus flagelliformis*), 97

Rauwolfia, 67
religious meanings, for botanical names, 28–35
reproduction, 45–46, 47
responses of plants, 100–102
Rhododendron spp. (rhododendron; azalea), 69
Rohdea japonica, 16
Roman topiary, 69
root pressures, 39
roots: decision making and, 41; directional sense
   of, 38; downward growth, 102–103; taking,
   37–39
rose, 34
rosemary (*Rosmarinus officinalis*), 63
Roxb. ex Hornem (*Macrophyllus*), 82
Rubus coronarius, 31
Rubus dumetorum, 31
Rubus ulmifolius, 31
rue, 27
rushes, 91

S

sacred trees, 86
saguaro cactus (*Cereus giganteus*), 18
Salvia sclarea (clary sage), 62
scaly bromeliad (*Aechmea pubescens*), 27
scarlet bergamot (*Mondara didyma*), 63
scarlet lily (*Lilium chalcedonicum*), 32
scents, deceitful, 53
Scotch heather (*Calluna vulgaris*), 49
sea cabbage (*Brassica oleracea*), 64
sea pink (*Armeria maritima*), 48
seaside daisy (*Erigeron glaucus*), 119
sedges, 58
seeds, 56–59; fast-growing, 59; germination, 56;
   slingshot, 57; transportation of, 58–59;
   travelling, 57; waterborne, 57–58
Selenicereus macdonaldiae (night-blooming cereus),
   97
self-pollination, prevention of, 48
Semper Augustus, 75
Sempervivum soboliferum (houseleek), 118
sensing climbers, 104
sepals, 50
Sequoiadendron (giant sequoia), 17–18
sexual reproduction, 46
shamrock, 35
Shasta daisy, 21, 23
shepherd's purse (*Capsella bursapastoris*), 42
shield fern (*Polystichum dudleyi*), 42
shittah tree, 28
short-day plants, 72–73
skunk cabbage, 21
smell, importance of, 55
Smithiantha (templebells), 52
smoke tree (*Dalea spinosa*), 27
snail flowers, 16
soil, 8, 40; dangerous minerals of, 44; topsoil,
   40–41
Solanum tuberosum (Irish potato), 69
Sorbus spp., 86
"soul-carrier" trees, 86

South American tree cactus (*Ceres chilensis*), 43
soybeans, 44
Spanish moss (*Tillandsia usneoides*), 37, 98
species names, 22–23
spores, 47, 105, 112–113
spread of plants, 6
stamen, 45, 48
Stapelia, 53
Stenomesson, 64
stigma, 36, 45
stomata, 94
strawberry, 35
Stropha belladonna, 70
style, 45
suberin, 84
succulents, 36, 92
sugar beets, 44
sunflower (*Helianthus*), 27
sweet balsam (*Melissa officinalis*), 26
syconium, 120
Sygzygium aromaticum (clove), 66
symbiosis, fungal, 113

T

talking, to plants, 101
tallest grass, 91
Taraxacum officinale (dandelions), 57–58
taro root, 42
tea, 117–118
templebells (*Smithiantha*), 52
tendrils, 103
thea (*Camellia sinensis*), 80, 117–118
Theaceae, 80
Thevetia, 64
Thevetia pueruviana (yellow oleander), 69
threadworm, 40
thrips, 49
Thunberg, Carl P., 23
Tillandsia usneoides (Spanish moss), 37, 98
timber grasses, 90
timing, for pollination, 47–48
tips of plant, pinching back, 102
tomatoes, 54
topiary, 79
topsoil, 40–41
touch-me-not (*Impatiens noli-tangere*), 57
Tradescant, John, 23
transpiration, 108
trapping mechanisms, 53
travelling plants, 102–104, 106–107
trees, 84–89; early, 17; fastest-growing, 89; first,
   16; fruit, first, 17; of gods, 87; largest living,
   17–18; northernmost, 18; oldest, 17; oldest
   living, 18; showiest, 89; transformations, 17;
   true, 86
Trichocereus candicans, 96
Trichocereus grandiflora, 111
Tripogandra grandiflora, 49
Tropaeolum, 64
tropism, 102

true trees, 86
tulips, 74–75
Typha latifolia (cattail), 10

U

Ulex europaeus (gorse), 57
Umbelliferae cuminum (cumin), 64–65

V

Valeriana officinalis (garden heliotrope), 27
The Various Contrivances by Which Orchids Are Fertilized by Insects, 15
vegetation, early, 9
Verbascum thapsus (flannel plant), 21
vibrations of plant, meaningful, 100–101
Victoria amazonica (giant water lily), 110
Violaceae, 22
violet, 66
viper's bugloss (*Echium plantagineum*), 73–74
von Linne, Carl, 22

W

Wake Robin, 21
walking fern (*Camptosorus rhizophyllis*), 105–106
walnuts, 90
water: cactuses and, 94–96; roots and, 39
water lily (*Nelumbo*), 32
water plants, adaptation to land, 5–6
weeds, 73–74
Weigel, C.E., 23

weigela, 23
western thistle (*Cirsium occidentale*), 23
wheat, 35
white bean, 29
white marguerite (*Chrysanthemum frutescens*), 33
Whitsun rose, 83
willow, 35, 116
winter, roots and, 38
Wisteria, 69
World tree, 86
wormwood (*Artemesia absinthium*), 116–117

X

Xanthorrhoea, 17
xerophytes, 92
Xerxes, 85
xylem, 84

Y

yam, 28
yellow asphodel (*Asphodeline lutea*), 63
yellow oleander (*Thevetia pueruviana*), 69
yew, 35
Yggdrasil, 86
yucca (*Hesperoyucca*), 19, 50–51

Z

zinc, 44
Ziziphus rhamnus christi (jujube), 65